IF THEY TOOK THE MUSIC AWAY... WOULD YOU *STILL* FOLLOW JESUS?

Let Those Who Have Ears to Hear

IF THEY TOOK THE MUSIC AWAY... WOULD YOU *STILL* FOLLOW JESUS?

Let Those Who Have Ears to Hear

Kimberly Smith

WINEPRESS WP PUBLISHING

Printed in the United States of America

Packaged by WinePress Publishing, PO Box 428, Enumclaw, WA 98022. The views expressed or implied in this work do not necessarily reflect those of WinePress Publishing. Ultimate design, content, and editorial accuracy of this work are the responsibilities of the author.

Unless otherwise noted, all Scriptures are taken from the King James Version of the Holy Bible.

Verses marked NKJV are taken from the *New King James Version*. Copyright © 1979, 1980, 1982 by Thomas Nelson, Inc. Used by permission. All Rights Reserved.

ISBN 1-57921-318-9
Library of Congress Catalog Card Number: 00-105879

ACKNOWLEDGMENTS

Many thanks to family and friends who provided a prayer base during the writing of this book. One dear friend even ran errands and cooked meals for us. Thank you!

Thanks to my children, for helping me have time to write and for making me laugh.

And a special thanks to my husband—mentor and best friend—whose support and encouragement have caused this book to become a reality.

CONTENTS

For do I now persuade men, or God? or do I seek to please men? for if I yet pleased men, I should not be the servant of Christ.

—Galatians 1:10

INTRODUCTION

T he screams, the cries of anguish, the *anger*—all gener-
ated by my first book, *Oh, Be Careful Little Ears*. Obviously the message hit the mark! I gave many radio interviews
across the nation—some were tension-filled, some were very
relaxed, and some were a true blessing to my heart. All in
all, the Lord carried me through with a deep sense of joy,
even though my heart was grieved many times.

I wasn't at all convinced God wanted me to write another book, until a series of events led me to consider the
idea. I even had in mind the final phrase with which to end
the last chapter. Therefore, when my husband said, "Here's
the title of your new book . . ." and (unknowingly) pro-
ceeded to state the exact same phrase, I knew God was calling me to write again.

I consider this the companion book to *Oh, Be Careful
Little Ears*. While my first book laid the groundwork, looking at contemporary Christian music (CCM) from both historical and biblical perspectives, this new book is a result of
questions people had during radio interviews, as well as my
own observations and insights during these past three years.
If you haven't already read the first book, it briefly tells the
history of Western civilization music (did you know it began in the early church?) and how CCM became accepted

into the modern-era Church. Biblically, it challenges the validity of contemporary Christian music, through specific verses as well as through scriptural principles God has given us for Christian living.

The subject of Christian music in general, and CCM in particular, is a touchy subject. Do you know why? It's simply because music is so inextricably tied to our emotions.

Music can make us feel energized. It can bore us. It can excite us and make us want to hop around in joy. It can make us feel melancholy, or it can inspire us to achieve our best.

So who wants to give up such a source of comfort to our souls? Who wants to give up something that has such power to lift us from depression or that can soothe our hectic day? Certainly not I.

Do you see how music is so tied to our emotions? And when something is so intertwined with our lives, our thoughts, our feelings, our experiences, wouldn't it be very difficult to give it up? To change our attitudes about? You'd better believe it. That is why it has become a subtle tool in Satan's hands—a tool by which he has effectively placed a Trojan horse into the midst of Christianity to undermine the very tenets of our Christian faith.

In this new book, I'll answer such questions as "How do you know *you're* right?" and "Shouldn't we be like Paul who was 'all things to all people'?" I'll also answer those Scriptures used in defense of CCM. And you'll read my personal testimony in chapter five.

Let me warn you: This book is not for those who don't want to hear the truth. Much like Paul's declaration that he "would not have known sin except through the law" (Rom. 7:7 NKJV), this book explains in detail the problems with CCM so that we will be aware of them. And *only* when we are aware of certain problems in our lives can we truly begin to deal with them as God desires—we *will* be accountable.

Some of you reading this will "have ears to hear." Some of you will want to "cast stones" (verbally or mentally). And some of you will be indifferent. In which category will you be?

It is my prayer that hearts and lives will change for God's glory.

KIM

PLEASE NOTE: Additional notes are indicated by *letters* and are included at the end of each chapter. *Numbers* identify reference endnotes, which can be found at the back of the book.

WHAT'S WRONG
WITH THIS PICTURE?

"As in water face reflects face,
So a man's heart reveals the man."
Proverbs 27:19 NKJV

A sweet elderly lady waits for the stoplight to turn so that she can cross the street. While she is waiting, however, a car full of youths pulls up next to her. While they don't seem to be causing any trouble, she's concerned. Rap music blares from the open windows, and the kids are "jammin'." Just last week her neighbor's house was broken into by a couple of delinquent teenagers, and she has always equated loud rock music with rebellion and crime. Finally, the car turns and drives away, and the lady breathes a sigh of relief.

What's wrong with this picture? The music blaring from the car was Christian rap, yet the dear lady couldn't distinguish it from secular rap. I guess God knows the hearts of the youths in that car, but the lady couldn't know. The messages sent through the musical style caused her worry and fear. I don't know about you, but as a Christian, I don't want to be thought of as someone who might intentionally cause another person physical or emotional harm. Yet that's exactly how these Christian youths were perceived.

It's mixed messages such as this that permeate the music world of Christianity in the twenty-first century. Do we belong to the world, or do we belong to God? Which is it to be? How can the secular world know for sure? Are *we* certain of where we belong?

As described in detail in my first book, *Oh, Be Careful Little Ears*, it's the appeal of most contemporary Christian music (CCM) to our carnal self, called our flesh in Scripture,[1] that makes it unacceptable, either as a representation of a Holy God, or as a method to impart spiritual truths to other believers. It's this appeal to the flesh, together with the "good" lyrics, that sends a mixed message to unbelievers and believers alike.

One doesn't have to have a music degree to understand how certain types of music appeal to our flesh. Pagans in undeveloped countries have exhibited basic understanding of the relationship between movement and music for centuries. Test the music for yourself: Turn on your favorite upbeat CCM. *Ignoring the lyrics,* stand up and "feel" the music in your body. How does it make you want to move? Does the music make you want to thrust out your head, or a shoulder, or your hips? Exaggerate the movements to better understand your response to the music. Do you feel pure in your spirit? Would you want to move like this before a Holy God?

Next, for contrast and purposes of illustration, turn to the classical music station on the radio. Now how does your body want to move? You should experience a noticeable difference in both body and spirit. Most notably, your torso (e.g., hips and shoulders) will for the most part remain still.

I was a guest on a radio program and someone called in, laughing at my statement that a pelvic thrust was a sensual movement. Are *you* laughing? God certainly isn't; in fact, Scripture condemns lewd behavior.[2] And yet this type of movement is exhibited all over the place in Christian concerts, crusades, youth events, and even churches. Oh, it may not be overt, but it's there. Why? Because the music, CCM in its many forms, with the underlying sensual beat, appeals to our flesh, whether or not the words are pure Scripture.

Certainly, I don't expect anyone to be thinking sensual thoughts because of CCM.[A] However, the type of response our bodies would like to make to this music *does* indicate that there's a problem. Does music that causes a person to "shimmy" or "thrust" present a true picture of a Holy God to unbelievers? Are shimmies and thrusts (whether restrained or not) a godly response to the music?

While this discussion may appear a bit crass, it is necessary if we are to understand, in the most simplistic of terms, the inappropriateness of most CCM for worship, evangelism, and praise to a Holy God. Whether or not we actively participate in movement of some sort to such music, the fact remains that the many styles of CCM, with their underlying rhythms and beats, *contribute* to the feeding of our flesh, rather than help us learn to deny it.

What has caused the controversy and confusion about Christian music? Lack of a basic understanding about how music affects us, and a further lack of sensitive discernment in the musical realm. Lack of complete biblical application using the whole counsel of Scripture. And, perhaps at the very root of the controversy is the lack of denial of our carnal, fleshly self. Each of these has added to the controversy in one way or the other. No longer, however, is it just a controversy. Our acceptance of CCM has resulted in many ramifications to the Church-at-large, to be discussed in later chapters.

Recently, I walked into a church sanctuary that perfectly pictures what has happened in many churches across America. Front and center stage was the drum set. To its right, four microphone stands; on the left, the electric piano. I finally noticed the Lord's Table, carefully placed at an angle on the right side of the podium to provide visual balance for the piano. When my eleven-year-old daughter asked if that was their Lord's table, I said, yes, and then asked her if she thought that the Lord's table should be off to the side, or in the center. "Now that I think about it, it should be in the center," she replied.

Traditionalists? Legalists? No. Admittedly, Scripture doesn't designate the placement of furniture in our New Testament churches as it did for the Tabernacle and Temple. It seems, however, that we would *want* to place the Lord's Table—as well as the pulpit from which the Word is preached—to symbolically indicate the honor and attention we give God in our worship: front and center.[B] But because of our lack of understanding and our unwillingness to deny our flesh in the area of music, the subtle message given by the arrangement of furniture in this church (a message many churches also convey solely through the use of CCM), whether or not we want to hear it, is: *Entertainment* and self-glory have replaced reverence and fear of the Lord in our worship services.

Will you have "ears to hear"?

Chapter One Notes

A. While sensual thoughts may not initially be a part of our response to CCM, the suggestiveness of a performer's body language and/or vocal inflections can lead our thoughts astray.

B. A study of the Tabernacle and Temple will reveal amazing symbolism in the placement of the furniture.

CHAPTER TWO

THE VOICE OF THE HARLOT

*"The mouth of an immoral woman is a deep pit;
He who is abhorred by the LORD will fall there."*
Proverbs 22:14 NKJV

Marilyn Monroe once sang *Happy Birthday* to President Kennedy. If you've ever seen a film clip of this event, aside from the revealing dress she wore, the manner in which she sang *Happy Birthday* is worth noting. In fact, she barely sang it; it was more of a breathy whisper.

Dr. Frank Garlock of Majesty Music makes an interesting point in his video series, *The Language of Music*: Would any woman want her husband to be spoken to by another woman in the tone of voice such as this? Sometimes vocalists also use a gravelly sound, and very often, they "scoop up" or "slide down" to a note instead of hitting it dead on.

These are all very sensual and suggestive techniques. "Loose," as in a "loose woman," implies that morals have become lax. Vocal techniques that don't adhere to pure and righteous standards of singing are also lax, or loose. Men vocalists use the same sensual techniques, and I seriously doubt that most husbands would want their wives to have a conversation with a man who uses them.

Yet we allow, and listen to, these techniques; we defend and applaud them in our Christian music, even in our worship services. Can this be pleasing to a Holy God? Dr. Garlock rightly identifies such techniques as "the voice of the harlot."[1] Proverbs 5:3 explains her voice this way: "For the lips of an immoral woman drip honey, And her mouth is smoother than oil" (NKJV). It's not the physical lips and mouth to which the Scripture is referring here; it's what comes out of her mouth and *how* she delivers her invitation. She is certainly not going to be speaking in a harsh tone of voice, nor is she going to be speaking in the same tone of voice someone would use to pray, either publicly, or privately. Most definitely, the voice of the harlot—her technique—is a sensual technique.

In the broader sense, the phrase, "voice of the harlot," not only refers to the vocal inflections of the artist, but can also be applied to most contemporary Christian music as a whole, as we'll soon discover.

I've often been asked how I define contemporary Christian music, and it's a valid question. Down through the ages, God's people have always been concerned about new developments in music, fearing these new developments were sensual. Each generation had its own new music which was considered contemporary at that time. More often than not, each new generation's music was an answer (a reaction) to the music that had gone before. The new music was a reflection of the times and what was going on morally, socially, and historically. No wonder good Christian people were always concerned, and perhaps a bit confused, about how to define *sensual*, and what was appropriate music for the Church. New musical innovations were often suspect to their way of thinking.

For example, did you know that in medieval times, the minor fifth (also known as a tritone, which is simply playing a *C* on the piano and then playing an *F* sharp) was strictly forbidden to be used in the Church? They called this the "devil's interval."[2] As interesting and as ridiculous as that may seem, it's just one example of the continuing debate over appropriate music for Christians. What everyone has failed to realize, though (both then and now), is that new musical techniques are not always sensual. They may delight and challenge our *intellect*, but this sensual experience must not be confused with those techniques that cross the line and appeal to our baser physical senses, as most of today's contemporary music does. *This is the crux of the debate.*

In the previous chapter, I suggested that a comparison be made between CCM and most any classical music.[A] While both types of music can cause a physical response, the response is vastly different. Toe tapping along with a melody is a righteous response: pelvic thrusts and shoulder shimmies are not. Why does the body want to respond differently?

It's simply because most classical music stimulates the *intellect* through harmonization, orchestration, or the counterpoint of J.S. Bach, for example, and we might tap our toes in response to the *melody* (the part we hum). Much of today's CCM, however, appeals to the *carnal/physical* through specific techniques such as offbeat drum rhythms that have been taken directly from secular rock music, and we'll respond to those offbeat rhythms *instead of* the melody—usually with carnal (sensual) body movements.

Therefore, CCM, as defined in twenty-first century terms, is any Christian music (regardless of the lyrics) that appeals to our carnal self by use of specific, identifiable, offbeat rock rhythms, sensual vocal inflections, and/or other carnal music techniques.[B] And because of this appeal to our flesh, most CCM—just like its secular counterpart, rock music—can rightly be called "the voice of the harlot." For in the final analysis, what else does a harlot appeal to?

Ezekiel 28:1–19 tells the story of Satan (called the King of Tyrus), and how he had originally been given musical ability (v. 13) before he sinned against God. Ever since God cast him out of heaven, Satan has cunningly tried to thwart and deceive God's people.

Now I'm not suggesting that all music is of Satan, far from it. But it's important to recognize that he is clever and musically creative and whispers deceitfully to us, knowing all the while that there are some forms of music that are not pleasing to God and that do not glorify Him.

Little do we realize how we have fallen in with Satan's plans to rob God of the glory and honor due Him when we use sensual music in our worship. Satan has been successful in that he's caused us to shift the focus of our worship from the spiritual/intellectual to the physical/emotional. We may think we've moved closer to God, but in actuality, we've moved further away. With each generation we've decayed, bit by bit.

You don't believe this? Look around at secular society. What kind of impact are Christians making? There used to be a day (as recently as when I grew up in the 1960's) when even unbelievers had a general respect for God and His people. Not anymore.

Oh, it may seem like we can "pack them in" at some churches with our programs and musicals and special events. But as the subtitle of my book suggests, if your church advocates the use of CCM, how many people would return to your church if the pastor decided there would be only traditional hymns with piano and organ accompaniment, or with no instruments at all? How long would it take for the congregation to dwindle in size?[C]

Indeed, the "voice of the harlot," represented through specific, identifiable techniques that please the flesh, is a powerful tool that appeals to many people, much like the tools used by advertisers to lure people to do things or go places they otherwise would not.

But should Christians use the same sensual music methods (or any tool) the world uses, in order to lure people to our churches? Would we allow our pastors to stand in the pulpit and deliver a sermon in a sensually suggestive voice along with sensually suggestive movements? Then why do we allow these behaviors during the music portion of our worship services? Why is there a difference?

Because, musically, we do not *want* to recognize the "voice of the harlot," having been willingly desensitized and deceived into thinking that the words are all that matter in our Christian music.

Chapter Two Notes

A. Sometimes classical music can also appeal to our flesh, particularly some music composed in the twentieth century (and beyond), because of the influence and use of carnal rhythms and techniques. We should test any and all music for adherence to scriptural principles and be spiritually alert for music that may actually be "technically" correct, but still contains spiritual darkness—as in New Age music, or the bizarre Gothic music/movement.

B. See Appendix Three for additional musical techniques that appeal to our flesh.

C. Chapter eight discusses how discerning Christians leave a church when CCM is introduced.

NOTE: Throughout this book, the term "rock music" refers to all genres of music that evolved—and continue to develop—out of early rock music. The term "CCM" refers to the various Christian counterparts of these styles of music, including CCM's very early forms, originally called "Jesus Music," then later, contemporary Christian music. (Jesus Music came out of the charismatic Jesus Movement, which began in the mid-1900's by relatively new Christians who mixed certain aspects of their youthful lifestyles [rock music] with elements of Pentecostalism.)

SPIRITUAL SONGS

*"Take away from Me the noise of your songs,
For I will not hear the melody of your stringed instruments."*
Amos 5:23 NKJV

Has your blood pressure reached the boiling point yet? It seems that when the subject of Christian music comes up, everyone rushes to his or her corner. This proves my point in the Introduction that the subject of Christian music is an emotional issue. It's right up there on the emotional meter with politics and abortion. Yet there are issues in life that don't cause such fervor. For example, the issue of driving above the speed limit.

The Bible clearly tells us that we are to obey the laws of our land.[1] Most of us feel convicted about speeding when we are reminded of these verses and appropriately modify our behavior—for awhile, anyway. We don't go to extremes to make excuses that speed limit laws don't apply to us because the Bible doesn't contain the words *speed limit*, and, therefore, we are exempt and can do what we like. Do you see how ludicrous this is?

Yet when the subject of music is involved, we heat up. We want to defend "our" music, and let no one tell us otherwise. We're emotionally tied to our music. Unlike the speeding issue, music is a hot-button issue in which we take great pains to guard our rights. Let's see if we can calm down, though, and look at what the Bible says about Christian music. Necessarily, this is a minor review for those who have read my first book. While I'm not going to go into the depth I did in *Oh, Be Careful Little Ears*, first-time readers need to take a quick look at Scripture and see what it has to tell us, and there are also new insights here that weren't included in my first book.

Before we go any further, we must remember that we are *not* discussing lyrics; that is entirely another subject. I understand that there are some truly meaningful lyrics that have recently been written, and I'm not disputing their validity. Although the lyrics are important, we must be aware that the musical vehicle carries its own message as well. In light of this fact, we will only be evaluating the musical vehicle and whether or not the vehicle of CCM meets biblical criteria.

There are two places in the New Testament where God specifically gives us instructions about the types of music that we are to use for worship and spiritual exhortation. Understand that when something is repeated in Scripture, we should pay careful attention. Near the end of Ephesians 5—in which the entire context is holy living—we read the following verse:

> Speaking to yourselves in psalms and hymns and spiritual songs, singing and making melody in your heart to the Lord. (Eph. 5:19)

And again, in Colossians:

> . . . teaching and admonishing one another in psalms
> and hymns and spiritual songs, singing with grace in
> your hearts to the Lord. (Col. 3:16)

In both of these Scriptures, we notice the phrase, "spiritual songs." Greek is a very precise language, and the particular Greek word here for *spiritual* is *pneumatikos*, meaning "non-carnal," and refers to our new, regenerate nature as Christians. The opposite of this is, of course, "carnal," meaning that part of our self that remains subject to sin's pull (also called our flesh).

Defined in the dictionary, *carnal* means:

1. Relating to the desires of the flesh; sensual.
2. Not spiritual.[2]

It makes sense, then, that when Paul used such a precise term—spiritual—to qualify the type of songs we are to sing as Christians, the original readers would have immediately understood that the Christian's music should help strengthen the new, regenerated spirit of a person, rather than appeal to his or her carnal self, manifested through a carnal, physical response to carnal music.

Their culture was replete with pagan worship, music, and drama, and the early Christians wisely avoided imitation of secular musical styles and instrumentation in order to help new Christians in their transition from their pagan past.[A] It would not have been enough for them to merely have good intentions, or motivations, in their music to God.

They understood the need to be "separate" in their worship style. They also understood that simply adding spiritual words did not make just any music "spiritual."

In twenty-first-century Christendom, however, we wish to interpret the phrase "spiritual songs" to mean that it only applies to the lyrics and our "inner motivation," or desire of the heart, not to any particular style. And, as the argument continues, God knows our hearts, and any offering to Him, accompanied by any style of music, is acceptable to Him. Offered from our spirits to God, any music (labeled "Christian") then becomes spiritual. It's the spirit in which the music is offered, not the actual musical style that matters.

Nothing could be further than the truth. It's exactly like saying all belief systems about how to get to heaven are acceptable to God, so long as people are sincere. Yet, just as God has given us instructions about true salvation, there are also principles He has given us that we can apply to music so that we can obey and please Him in our worship.

And that's exactly what worship is all about—pleasing and obeying God, not pleasing ourselves, in the music we create, as well as in the lyrics we write. Hence the phrase, "spiritual songs," with the qualifying word, "spiritual," meaning non-carnal (non-flesh-appealing) songs. It's as if God allowed us a broad brushstroke of creativity so that we may express ourselves, yet our personal expressions, culturally, as well as preferentially, should *every one* fall under the term "spiritual." That is to say, both the music and the lyrics should be encouraging to our new, regenerate nature, in stark contrast to appealing to our carnal self—freedom of creativity within limitations.

This is where the rubber meets the road in the realm of contemporary music for Christians, and I've been asked if my interpretation of the term "spiritual songs" can really be correct. Most definitely yes, because quite simply, our bodies will automatically "interpret" music in only two ways—carnally or non-carnally.

Carnal responses include a thrusting out of the hips or the head (like a chicken), a shimmy of the shoulders, or other independent, hip-swaying movements. Non-carnal responses would be any movements in which the torso remains fairly still, such as in marching, traditional folk dancing, square dancing, or ballet. While allowing that anything can be perverted, it's interesting to see that both of these movement categories basically require specific musical techniques in order to evoke either type of response.

So what are the specific techniques? For a carnal response, they are techniques used in jazz or rock music (with all of their various styles), and this undeniably includes most contemporary Christian music. Techniques, such as repetitious offbeat accents,[B] whether played by a drum or bass guitar (drum techniques which do not in any way support the melody of the musical piece, but are an entity of their own, even if the offbeat drum rhythm is subtly in the background). Strong, jazz-type rhythms that have been written into the melody, with or without a rhythm instrument, also appeal to our flesh.[C] *Anytime* offbeats are repetitiously accented (in a melody, or by means of a rhythm instrument), our bodies will respond with carnal (suggestive) movements. Likewise, when drums, or any other rhythm instrument, repetitiously dominate the melody by loudly accenting every beat (so that the drums are equal to, or greater than, the melody), this, too, is a very carnal appeal to our flesh.

We need to understand that rhythm itself is not wrong if used properly. Our words have rhythm, and a simple melody is rhythm applied to musical notes. Think of the song, *Happy Birthday*—that's a rhythm. We could change the rhythm, yet keep the same notes, and the entire "feel" of the song would be different.

For example, contrast the way Marilyn Monroe sensuously sang this song to President Kennedy, to the way it's sung at a child's birthday party. Rhythm is a powerful (and sometimes "suggestive") tool, and our bodies respond to it, righteously or unrighteously, depending upon the way the rhythm itself is employed—righteously or unrighteously. And when repetitious, offbeat drums are added, or when drums flagrantly dominate the music, another unrighteous, carnal dimension of rhythm is demonstrated by the very way we want to respond to those drumbeats, rather than the melody.

Other subtle appeals to our flesh were mentioned in chapter two—vocal techniques such as sliding or scooping (instead of hitting a note right on target), and breathiness or gravelliness. And while these vocal techniques may not necessarily cause a carnal body response, they are carnal nonetheless. Jazz music, a precursor of rhythm, rhythm and blues, and ultimately rock music, also commonly makes use of sliding, scooping, and "teasing," which is holding a note just a little bit longer than necessary.[D]

For music to be truly spiritual (non-carnal), the melody must be priority, with any other rhythms in full support and subjection to it. Traditional hymns are a prime example, and most classical orchestral music shows us that many instruments can contribute beautifully to a piece of music, while maintaining the integrity of the composition, by following the lead of the melody, and with all the separate parts using the first-beat-strong rule, even in baroque music, which is very "busy."

What about syncopation? The occasional use of *syncopation*, musical accents falling on a normally weak beat, is fine, but only if it's delivered crisp and clean and doesn't dominate the music; the repetitious use of an offbeat (rock) drum, however, is a misuse of syncopation, and, in my opinion, doesn't qualify as true syncopation. Carefully placed syncopation which supports the melody can make music lively and exciting. And just as in music that is played straight without accented offbeats, properly used syncopation will not cause sensual body movements: improper use of syncopation will (as in jazz, Dixieland, or rock music).

(For a complete discussion of syncopation, and to hear musical clips which demonstrate each of these sensual music techniques, I would suggest the audio taped seminar, *How to Evaluate Music*, by Pastor T.P. Johnson.[E])

Am I suggesting that everything recently written (everything contemporary) is carnal? Not at all. This is *not* an issue of contemporary music vs. traditional music. It's simply an issue of choosing non-flesh appealing music over music that does appeal to our flesh—*regardless of when the music was written*. Unfortunately, most (not all) contemporarily written Christian music (labeled CCM) does appeal to the flesh.

To completely fulfill the meaning of the term "spiritual songs" in Ephesians 5:19 and Colossians 3:16, music that we offer to God in worship must not appeal to the carnal self, either in lyric or in musical content. And because most CCM only meets *one* of those criteria (the lyrics), it does not present a valid style for Christian music; it's really only secular rock music with Christian lyrics—rock music which runs the gamut from "soft" rock to "alternative" and beyond.

There's no need to plow old ground about the evils of secular rock music; however, it is not redeemable for the Christian's use, as many people claim. Some things in life cannot be righteously adapted and must be left alone.[3] Only those things in life that haven't disregarded biblical principles in the first place (that haven't been born out of rebellion and are anti-Christian from inception) can be redeemed for the Christian's use.

For example, do you know if a Christian designed your clothing? Probably not, but if those clothes follow godly principles of modesty, they are acceptable for your use. What about television? Does the misuse of such technology through sinful programming invalidate television for the believer? No, God designed those electromagnetic waves in the first place, yet those same waves can be used by both Christians and unbelievers alike.

I discussed the early-hymn-writers-borrowed-tavern-music excuse in my first book.[F] Such music was redeemable, only because the simple melody was rewritten into a chorale form and adapted to the words of the hymn-poem. The actual tavern style was not imitated, and borrowing melodies was a very common practice at that time, anyway.

In all of these examples, the secular application could be adapted for the Christian's use because the basic quality of each illustration had not disregarded biblical principles in the first place; however, the style of rock music *has* violated biblical principles. And because this style of music was purposely rebellious and anti-Christian (anti-moral) from its inception, it is *not* redeemable for Christian music.

What type of music fulfills the full application of the phrase "spiritual songs"? Of course, hymns sung in the traditional style and most classical music.[G] Additionally, any music written contemporarily that doesn't use techniques that appeal to our carnal self.

As mentioned earlier, there have been some outstanding Christian lyrics and melodies written in these last few decades, and some contemporary Christian music which contains truly Christ-exhalting lyrics could be made to conform to biblical principles if the rock influence was removed and the vocalists sang "straight" (without any sensual vocal techniques).[H, I]

Wouldn't the meaning of the lyrics remain the same? In fact, the lyrics would be even *more* meaningful because both the message of the lyrics and the message of the music would be identical—righteous and truly spiritual, as far as humanly possible. Christian music being just that: Christian. And this is an important point for our evangelism efforts.

If our music is pure, as I've just described, we can rest assured that we've provided the optimum opportunity for unbelievers to hear from the Lord and make a life-changing decision without being influenced by flesh-appealing musical techniques. If we are providing carnal music, however, we cannot have this same confidence; we cannot be certain that people are not responding as a result of an external, momentary, exciting, musical stimulus. (Haven't we all felt as if we can conquer the world when we listen to certain music, only later to realize that this is not reality?)

So to summarize, the phrase "spiritual songs," as it should be translated from the Greek, properly applies not only to the words, but to the music itself, and complies with the whole counsel of Scripture regarding purity of life for the believer.

In contrast, the term "rock 'n' roll" has been called a "sexual metaphor,"[6, J] a term that not only refers to the lyrics, but also to the style of music with its specific, identifiable techniques that appeal to the baser, carnal proclivities of the listener.[K, L]

Over thirty years ago, rock musician Frank Zappa commented about the identifiable, repetitious beat: "To deny rock music . . . was to deny sexuality." He further quotes early rock music promoter Hal Zeiger's comment that, "the big beat matches the body's rhythms,"[10] and in the book, *The Legacy of John Lennon: Charming or Harming a Generation?* David Noebel concludes, "Rock 'n' roll is musical pornography."[11] And despite the secular world's acknowledgement that certain musical techniques appeal to our carnal, fleshly self, most contemporary Christian music uses these *same* identifiable, sensual techniques as the vehicle for its lyrics.

This is not in keeping with God's Word regarding holy living for the believer.[12] Therefore, because of its carnal nature, CCM does not comply with either of these two New Testament references to sing non-carnal songs, nor with the entire counsel of Scripture, which inclusively warns us away from sensual behavior and encourages us toward pure and holy living in every area of our lives.

Yet, while God has clearly told us that He desires for us to sing "spiritual (non-carnal) songs," as with any practice we don't want to give up, there are many justifications from man's perspective, and these will be addressed in the next chapter.

Chapter Three Notes

A. This is documented in my first book.

B. "Offbeats" (also called "backbeats," or "breakbeats") are the second and fourth beats in music that counts four beats to a measure. Rock music rhythm instruments (bass guitar, drums, etc.) apply a strong emphasis to these beats, whereas in classical music, the strong beats fall on the first and third beats in four/four time, or the first beat of three/four time, with or without percussion. (This includes traditional hymns and most all Western civilization music up until about the time of very early jazz [c. 1900], out of which evolved such musical styles as swing, big band, rhythm and blues, rock, etc.)

C. A recognizable song that uses a strong, carnal (jazz) rhythm in the melody is "Cruella DeVil" from the animated version of the movie, *101 Dalmatians*.

D. Sliding, scooping, and teasing are very subtle sensual techniques that can be understood as we gain further discernment. See chapter nine. Also see Appendix Three for additional techniques which are designed to appeal to our flesh.

E. Refer to Appendix One, "Tapes and Videos," for more information.

F. See pages 84–86 of *Oh, Be Careful Little Ears* for a complete and documented discussion of the excuse that Martin Luther set his hymns to the worldly songs of his day.

G. The development of Western civilization music—classical music—is traced back to the New Testament Church.[4]

H. Tim Fisher and Dan Sweatt, in the audio tape series, *Praise Him in Joyful Song*, point out that when a vocalist uses sensual techniques, the attention is drawn to the vocalist, whereas when the vocalist sings straight, the attention is drawn to the words of the music, and then ultimately to God.[5] It should also be noted that when a person attracts attention to himself through these sensual vocal techniques, he or she has robbed God of the glory He deserves and has taken it for him or herself.

I. Also refer to Appendix One for additional musical styles which follow biblical parameters for music—both secular and sacred.

J. A much more explicit term than "sexual metaphor" has been used for the phrase, "rock and roll," and rock and roll also implied "both sex and wild partying."[7]

K. Richard Aquila in his book, *That Old Time Rock and Roll,* quotes an interview of Bill Haley in which he explains that any piece of music could be changed so that listeners would be able to dance to it, specifically, how the accents were dropped from the first and third beats and placed on the second and fourth beats, also adding a beat people could dance to.[8] (Bill Haley was one of the key influencers/developers of the "new" sound of rock 'n' roll. Notice his reference to a specific technique employed to achieve the desired result—namely dancing.) NOTE: This was an uninhibited form of dancing in response to the new, uninhibited form of music. In direct contrast, God desires that we have self-control.[9]

L. Carnal rock music techniques are also prevalent in much modern-day **gospel/southern gospel music**—with its repetitious drumbeat, "walking" bass, and sometimes suggestive vocal techniques. Contemporary gospel/southern gospel may not appear as extreme as CCM simply because today's southern gospel is an old style jazzed up, whereas CCM is a worldly style embraced; however, both styles of music appeal to the flesh. But just as CCM could be cleaned up, contemporary gospel music could also be cleaned up to conform to God's Word regarding righteous music.

CHAPTER FOUR

WHAT WE BELIEVE
IS OUR "TRUTH"

"A wise man will hear, and will increase learning . . ."
Proverbs 1:5

Ahhh! The chapter we've all been waiting for—the continuation of my first book's chapter titled, "Excuses, Excuses." The following statements and questions were not covered in *Oh, Be Careful Little Ears* (with the exception of a couple that necessitated further explanation) and most are a result of actual interview comments and discussions which need to be addressed more fully.

Many of these ideas sound convincing on the surface, but we need to examine them in light of the whole counsel of Scripture, instead of forming our ideas on what we personally believe or pull out of selected Scriptures in order to support our position.

While some verses in the Bible can stand alone (i.e., John 3:16), all verses should be compared to similar verses as well as the whole counsel of Scripture. We must be very careful when trying to support any belief with only one or two Scriptures without looking at the whole of Scripture because we can easily get ourselves into a lot of trouble.

For example, Deuteronomy 6:4 says, "Hear, O Israel: The LORD our God is one LORD." If we take this at face value, there would be no room for the triune nature of God revealed throughout the whole of Scripture—in fact, it would appear to contradict the doctrine of the Trinity.

Yet, I commonly see this practice of "lifting" Scriptures for the defense of CCM, a practice that makes some arguments sound somewhat reasonable, but ignores other Scriptures and biblical principles that give fuller revelation, counsel, and balance. I also see the alarming practice of using our own reasoning as our final authority, rather than the Word of God.

Because this chapter is extremely long, I've provided a shorter answer in bold with the fuller explanation immediately following. Let me say at the outset that I'm aware that there are many sincere, Bible-believing Christians who love their CCM. My intention is not in any way to question anyone's salvation or the sincerity of their love for Christ Jesus. For the purpose of exposing CCM for what it really is, however, this chapter, and the following chapters, are very straightforward.

Remember, this is not a personal attack against individuals; the intention here is to examine the music that we've come to embrace as Christians. That said, now let's really examine these additional excuses, as well as the Scriptures used for promoting contemporary Christian music.

1. *People are saved at CCM concerts.*

Many people—including myself—have made "professions of faith" without true conversion. If some people are truly saved in the concert environment, it's only because God saves people *in spite of* the music, not because of it.

This is the old "the ends justifies the means" argument, and I would have to say that true salvation is the exception, rather than the rule, at CCM concerts.[A]

Even in God's Word we see that the reasoning behind this argument is not correct. Only God has the right to use whatever means He chooses to drive a message home to an individual. As Christians, we must not go beyond any parameters He gives us in His Word.

For example, Pharaoh's magicians spoke "truth" when they told him that God was sending the plagues.[2] Does this vindicate the use of evil magicians for spreading the gospel? Absolutely not, because we are told that enchanters, witches, wizards, magicians, etc. are an abomination to the Lord God.[3] What about Balaam's donkey that spoke to Balaam through God's providence?[4] Are we to venerate donkeys because of this incidence? No.

Probably every Christian has had some experience in everyday life that God has used to enlighten him or her about a spiritual truth. That does not mean we try to duplicate that experience for other people so they can "see" that truth also. We may share it, but we don't duplicate the experience.

If you are reading this and have received *true* salvation[B] as a result of attending a CCM concert, I am happy for your new life in Christ Jesus. But just as with the examples of the magicians or Balaam's donkey, the end does not justify the means for God's people—only for God Himself. We must answer to God; He does not answer to us.

2. *The music really makes me feel closer to God; it's a "spiritual" experience for me.*

An emotional experience is not necessarily a spiritual experience.

Feelings and emotions play a huge part in the realm of CCM. Certainly people can experience depth of feeling for God and get emotional, but people get emotional at secular rock concerts also. Does that mean they got "saved" or had a spiritual/religious experience? And many people who belong to cults, quasi-religions, and the New Age movement consider themselves spiritual, too.

Recently I attended a concert for piano and violin. There were moments when the music was so beautiful and spellbinding that it was very moving to the emotions. But it was not a *spiritual* experience! It was simply very moving. And last fall, my family visited the war memorials in Washington, DC. That was a moving, emotional experience also. But it was not a *spiritual* experience!

This is where Satan has confused many, many people—Christians and non-Christians alike. An emotional experience does not necessarily mean we've had a spiritual experience. Let me repeat: An emotional experience does not equal a spiritual/religious experience.

To write it as an equation:

EMOTIONAL EXPERIENCE $\neq$ SPIRITUAL EXPERIENCE.

Emotions are very unreliable spiritual "gauges" with many variables thrown in, such as our circumstances (did we suffer a recent loss of some sort?), hormonal imbalance, lack of sufficient vitamins in our diet, lack of sleep, etc.

Different musical styles also affect our emotions, and some music can evoke feelings and emotions that can be addictive to our carnal self.

Therefore, an emotional experience, whether in church, at a CCM concert, or anywhere else for that matter, does not necessarily mean we've been "saved" or had a religious experience. Our emotions do not save us. The Bible says we are saved through faith in Christ Jesus.[5]

Furthermore, a sensational emotional experience incited by a flesh-pleasing CCM concert does not put a person in the right frame of mind to understand what Jesus says in Mark 8:34: "Whosoever will come after me, let him deny himself, and take up his cross, and follow me." Salvation is a very serious decision and commitment, because if we truly mean business with God, our lives will change. And that change is not easy. In fact, Christians have it tough because we are now struggling against our carnal self instead of giving in to it.[6]

Yes, we may be grieved over our sins (I hope so); we may be joyful because of God's blessings; or we may have any number of emotions that result from God working in our lives. But valid emotions—such as these that result from our thinking about Him—can just as well come at any time other than listening to music.

It heartens me to hear about pastors across this country who are concerned that there can be conviction without true conversion. Likewise, there can be emotionalism without true salvation.

Yes, a spiritual experience can be emotional. But an emotional experience doesn't guarantee our experience was truly spiritual. So be very careful about the place you give emotions and/or feelings in your life, and be very careful not to depend upon music to get your spiritual "highs."

3. *Where in the Bible does it say a certain "beat" is wrong?*
Where in the Bible does it say we should wear a certain style of clothing? As soon as God would have said a certain beat is wrong, sinful man would have come up with other, flesh-pleasing beats and rhythms.

Direct commands ("Thou shalt not . . .") deal with *specific* sins common to man across the centuries. Scriptural principles may be applied broadly over the course of history as new innovations and cultural change dictate application to life circumstances that could not be addressed individually in Scripture.

God is no fool, which is why He has given us principles to guide us in those areas that are far-reaching. For example, I could dress in a nun's habit and still act immodestly. But as long as I dress and behave modestly (as I would dress if I were to meet Jesus face to face), I have followed scriptural principles. The same is true with music. Therefore, the principles given to us in Ephesians 5:19 and Colossians 3:16 are perfect, and they fit in with the whole counsel of Scripture. By using the term, "spiritual (non-carnal) songs," God has given a broad application of limitation to any musical style that might appeal to our carnal self that remains prone to sin.

Therefore, the term "non-carnal" gives us necessary parameters for our music, yet within those parameters, we are allowed the freedom of creativity and personal preference.

4. *Psalm 33:3 says to "play skillfully with a loud noise."*
Just because any particular music can be loud, loudness alone doesn't qualify it as fully complying with God's Word.

The key word here is *loud*, also found in a few other Old Testament references about singing and instrumentation,[7] and this statement is based on the supposition that CCM, with its microphones and amplifiers, fulfills this Scripture about (loud) praise.

This argument, however, does not take into account the *whole* counsel of Scripture. While CCM is loud, it still violates Ephesians 5:19 and Colossians 3:16, as well as other scriptural principles about holy living, because it appeals to the flesh. Conversely, when we use music that follows the biblical principles of these two New Testament verses (and the entire counsel of Scripture regarding holy living) we can—at the same time—also satisfy the Old Testament teachings of loudness (and exuberance).

A word of caution is in order: God never meant for us to overuse any means by which we could permanently damage our ability to hear, as has been the case with amplifiers, which is a scientifically proven fact. We greatly err when people in our church services complain or have to cover their ears because the music is so loud.

Loudness to the point of a painful experience for some people is not what God is indicating through these Scriptures. Neither is it demonstrating love and concern for fellow brothers and sisters in Christ. And there's something decidedly wrong if we have to "crank up" the music in order to have a worship experience.

5. *Psalm 33:3 also says that we're to sing "a new song" unto the Lord.*

The term "new song" does not refer to a musical style. CCM has been designated by some as the "new song" of our times. While CCM may be newer in style than traditional hymnody, this new style doesn't truly qualify it as a new song; it still violates scriptural principles for Christian music.

When we become new in Christ Jesus,[8] then, and only then, we can sing a new song. It's a song of the redeemed; it's not a musical style. Hence, verses such as Psalm 144:9 and 149:1; Revelation 5:9 and 14:3. And this one, from Isaiah 51:11: "Therefore the redeemed of the LORD shall return, and come with singing unto Zion; and everlasting joy shall be upon their head . . . ."

As new creatures in Christ Jesus, our song—our new life message, with praise given to God for our redemption—is new. And in keeping with our new (transformed) life, our music should also reflect that transformation by conforming to biblical standards, both lyrically and musically. This is a true "new song."

6. *I don't feel sensual when I listen to CCM.*

Of course, you don't; this is a mistake people make when I refer to CCM as sensual music. The emotion of sensuality (i.e. lust, with its physical ramifications) is differentiated from the immediate physical (movement) response we have to either secular rock or Christian rock music.

Emotion and physical response are two separate conditions, and they cannot be used interchangeably as they apply to CCM. One may lead to the other; for example, I'm sad (emotion), so I cry (physical response). Any music (even classical music) can be passionate (meaning that the music is played with intense feeling) at times.

When I refer to CCM as being sensual, I mean that it uses techniques that appeal to our carnal self, although we don't recognize them as such until we gain discernment. So when we test CCM by evaluating the physical movements our body naturally wants to make to such music, we do, indeed, see that our movements *are* sensual in form. We are not feeling the emotion of sensuality, but we *are* demonstrating the carnal effect the music has on our bodies.

As we become more and more discerning in the musical realm, however, we will actually perceive in our spirits the sensuality of certain musical techniques.

7. *What's wrong with "dancing before the* LORD"? *It's biblical.*

The Old Testament Hebrew words for dancing, such as *raqad* and *karar*, really mean jumping, stamping, or whirling, not the sensual dancing we are familiar with today.

I covered this to some degree in my first book, and, unfortunately, Old Testament passages about dancing[9] are used as an excuse for today's Church to engage in (sensual) dancing or movement as part of worship.

Unlike God's specific, orderly instructions for the Levitical musicians and singers, *nowhere* do we see specific instructions for dancers or dancing during corporate worship. In fact, whenever God's glory appeared in the Temple, the Bible says that the people "stood."[10]

Now I'm not suggesting that spontaneous hand-clapping, or toe-tapping, as a joyful response to an uplifting, non-carnal melody, is wrong. But when David danced before the Ark, he did not by any stretch of the imagination (or context of the passage) participate in pelvic thrusts or any other sensual movements in response to sensual music techniques—all of which are prevalent in our day. Not in any single biblical passage, referring to dancing as part of our praise to God, do we see such a display. Rather, we might imagine a jump for joy, a skip, stomping, a "round" dance, or a type of whirling or twirling. These are truer meanings of the Hebrew text.

For a more in-depth discussion about dancing and its role in the modern Church, I would suggest the book, *Harmony at Home* by Tim Fisher.[11] Mr. Fisher gives this subject a close look as it applies to worship, and makes many enlightening points.

His conclusion, as well as mine, is: If a person wants to express his or her spontaneous joy in private, as a result of God's blessing, by whirling, marching, or jumping, that is fine. The corporate, sensual type of dancing in response to the rock music in today's churches, however, bears no resemblance to Old Testament (Hebrew) forms of dancing, and, furthermore, is unbiblical. For how could we even consider that sensually suggestive movements such as shoulder shimmies, pelvic thrusts, or hip-swaying movements glorify and praise a Holy God? And how do these types of movements exhibit self-control, which is a fruit of the Spirit?

8. *The movements I make are only little knee bounces; I'm not thrusting any parts of my body.*

Exaggerate those movements and use the aid of a full-length mirror.

Can you keep your torso stiff from your shoulder to the top of your thigh (like a board) and bounce your knees? (No waist movement!) If you can, you are now doing a movement similar to a ballet's *plié* (pronounced plee-ay), and your head will also descend. This is very difficult to do if the music is upbeat.

From the little pelvic thrusts to the full-out pelvic thrusts, they are both of the same genre: sensual movement. If someone exhibited this behavior in public, without music, we would say that the person was demonstrating lewd behavior. But we are not making the connection when music is involved; we have become desensitized. *Our desensitization does not make lewd behavior OK in God's eyes.* He condemns it![12] Because we have been so desensitized to body movements, however, the little pelvic movements, which go along with little knee bounces, can actually seem clean and harmless. But when compared to the movements of ballet or traditional folk dancing, which keep the torso straight, there is definitely a difference we need to acknowledge and address.

Perhaps, however, you honestly don't move in a sensually suggestive fashion to such music. Maybe you simply tap your toes to the music. Yet, it bears repeating that toe-tapping to the additional offbeat drum rhythm, *instead of* the melody, still indicates that the music is appealing to the flesh, rather than edifying the spirit/intellect.

Our spirits/minds respond to the melody; our bodies respond to the rhythm. When a melody is the priority, with no repetitious offbeat accents, our spirits/minds will respond first—our bodies will respond secondary. If the rhythm is the priority, through a dominating drumbeat, repetitious, offbeat drums, or repetitious offbeat rhythms in a melody, our bodies will respond first—with our emotions (not spirits) secondary. God wants us to be spiritually discerning—not carnally stimulated by musical techniques which appeal to the flesh.

And while there's nothing wrong with rhythm in its rightful place, and nothing wrong with a righteous physical response (i.e. hand-clapping or toe-tapping) to a righteously played non-carnal melody, out-of-balance and/or out-of-place rhythms, which do not support a melody, will encourage improper body movements and "feed the flesh."

Yet, simply addressing our body movements is just the tip of the iceberg. We could hold our bodies as stiff as a ramrod while the music was playing, but the underlying sensual music techniques used in CCM (which cause these wrong body responses) would still be there.

That is the issue that must be addressed!

9. *Dance movements are only cultural expressions of movement to each culture's music. There are no right or wrong dance movements.*

A pelvic thrust is a pelvic thrust in any culture, and God doesn't change scriptural principles for each culture.

As mentioned in my first book, every culture would have examples of carnal and non-carnal music, even if it was not a Christian culture. Some cultural music is more carnal (African, Jamaican, etc.); some cultures have a more non-carnal-type music (traditional music of Japan and China; Scottish and Irish folk music, etc.).

Pelvic thrusts, or hip swaying, *are* sensual movements, no matter how we try to excuse them.

10. *Both Jesus and Paul "met people where they were."*

Jesus and Paul might have "met people where they were" in those people's understanding of life at that moment (the Samaritan woman at the well, the idolaters of Athens, etc.),[13] but they *never* adopted the sinful practices of the people they were trying to reach.

While CCM might, through a few lyrics, provide a moment of "connection" for the listener, in a genre unbelievers can relate to (flesh-pleasing music), this does not vindicate the use of CCM. Although some CCM songs do have meaningful lyrics, the fact still remains that the musical techniques are gratifying the flesh, whether we recognize it or not. This is most certainly *not* "meeting people where they are." In reality, this is validating the unbelievers' present lifestyle of feeding their flesh and their emotions; this is not teaching them that the true Christian life is a life of denial of our flesh, as we strive toward holiness in obedience to our Lord, Whom we love.[14]

To properly and biblically meet people where they are, we need to understand them individually, offering hope that is only found in Jesus Christ, no matter their circumstance. We should also demonstrate that we love and care for people by clothing them and feeding them, if necessary, recognizing their needs of the moment.

And most importantly, we need to live out a changed life, depending on the sustaining grace of the Lord Jesus Christ, so that they can *see* that what we are talking is real, even when our own life is tough.

But if Christians are musically imitating the very forms of sinful techniques and wrong attitudes that unbelievers hear on a day-to-day basis from secular music, we are certainly not modeling a *changed* life in Christ.

Imitation of sinful habits is not what is meant by the phrase "meeting people where they are." The Bible strongly tells us to, "cleanse ourselves from all filthiness of the flesh and spirit, perfecting holiness in the fear of God" (2 Cor. 7:1).

How can we, who are to "perfect holiness," in good conscience use the *very same* sensual music techniques that secular artists use in their rock/alternative music? How can we, who are to "cleanse ourselves from all filthiness of the flesh," in good conscience then sensually dance to CCM as the unbeliever's dance to secular rock music?

Meeting people where they are is a concept that is valid only on a personal, one-on-one basis. As Christians, we are to introduce people to Jesus Christ, Who is the only One Who can perfectly meet people "where they are."

But we *cannot* introduce people to our beloved Lord Jesus Christ through a sensual medium (CCM) because the true gospel of Jesus Christ is not a sensual gospel. And God is not a "sensual" God.

11. *Music is amoral.*

Were you aware that this argument was initiated by *Christians* in an effort to defend CCM? Secular authors have proved otherwise.

Book after book has been written by secular authors who demonstrate that music *is* moral, or immoral, depending upon the techniques used to create a message. These authors further show that rock music seeks to focus on the sexual— seeks to create sensual body movements in the listener by the use of specific musical techniques apart from the lyrics—and some authors cite rock musicians who readily (and crudely) admit this.[15] *CCM uses the very same techniques.*

If we believe that music is amoral, then we must answer this question: Why do some musical styles cause us to move our bodies in sensual movements, while other types of music do not?

Therefore, while I would agree that a musical note by itself is amoral, the way we arrange them in specific rhythms (along with other musical techniques) ultimately defines whether or not the final piece of music is moral or immoral, regardless of the lyrics.

12. CCM concerts are great tools for evangelism.

No, because the draw and focus is the music, the individual performer, or the group, not Jesus Christ. The whole concert concept is to have a good time, not get serious about spiritual things.

Evangelism is probably the number one excuse (the "umbrella" under which most other excuses fall) that we use in order to justify CCM. We act like music is our only tool for evangelism. It's our drawing card, so to speak, and then we can share the gospel (so we believe).

Yes, there are some performers who take evangelism seriously. This is commendable; however, the use of music that contains flesh-pleasing techniques must still be considered. And we must use caution when evangelizing, as well. We must be extremely careful that we are not misrepresenting Christianity or our Lord Jesus Christ in any manner.

It's easy to get people to "make decisions" in the electric atmosphere of a concert when the mood has been musically set and people are riding the wave of emotionalism, either feeling like they can conquer the world, or the opposite, feeling melancholy. Making a decision to become followers of Christ is very serious, however, and not to be taken lightly, or while in the throws of musically-induced emotionalism. Furthermore, there must be a clear presentation of the gospel, along with an individual's personal conviction that her or she is a sinner in need of a Savior, before anyone can experience true salvation.

Listen to the words of Jesus, speaking about becoming a disciple: "For which of you, intending to build a tower, does not sit down first and *count the cost*, . . ." (Luke 14:28 NKJV, emphasis mine).[16]

Is it really possible to count the cost of being a true disciple of Christ, and all that goes with it, in the electrically-charged atmosphere of most CCM concerts? (An atmosphere that is also experienced at secular rock concerts.)

For purposes of illustration, let's contrast people's behavior and the atmosphere of two events: a CCM concert and a presentation of Handel's *Messiah,* specifically the "Hallelujah Chorus." I think most of us can easily see the difference. The CCM concert will have fancy lights, staging, and possibly dancing; teenagers may be running up and down the aisles or standing in their seats. They may even take part in "moshpits."[c] Conversely, while the "Hallelujah Chorus" is being performed, most people, including teenagers, stand quietly out of reverence for God.

Which concert more effectively directed the listeners' attention toward Almighty God? Which concert commanded their respect? And which concert most accurately demonstrated the holiness of God? Yet they *both* had lyrics about the Lord Jesus Christ.

If CCM concerts and music are so effective in evangelism, where are the changed lives as testimony? There should be thousands. Our world should be drastically changing for the better. Do you see it happening? I certainly don't. What I do see is mass, temporary Christianity. Feel-good Christianity with a moshpit mentality. Worldly Christianity. *Mediocre Christianity.*

These are not true representations of biblical Christianity because there is a cost to following Jesus.

Consequently, at CCM concerts, as well as in churches that regularly use contemporary Christian music, the Church is demonstrating that there is no real cost to following Jesus. CCM makes people comfortable in their lifestyle, and there is not a large enough chasm between it and the world's sound to truly exhibit musically how far short they fall and how much they need a Savior. As a result, what is really happening is that many people are joining the "club"; however, they're *not* really joining the true family of God.

In the frenzy of an "alternative" CCM concert, for example, do the unbelievers see scriptural truths lived out? They don't. Take away the music, take away the distraction of the dancing and lights, take away the glamour, and the truth will be revealed.

For when the last microphone plug is pulled, and contemporary Christian music's "evangelism" efforts are revealed by fire,[17] will there be a reward for the use of identifiable, carnal music techniques in order to reach people for Jesus?

I don't think so.

13. *Paul and Silas sang hymns in prison and people were saved.*

Paul and Silas sang hymns as an act of praise in their time of personal suffering, the result of which was that the witness of their faith *through a difficult time* drew others to Christ.

This refers to the account in Acts 16:16–34. Two lonely voices—praising God in the middle of the night after they had been whipped and thrown into jail—without a band, without a crowd, except a few other prisoners.

Let's think about this scenario. The inner prison is dark and probably filthy, filled with stench. It's midnight, and Paul and Silas are nursing serious, open sores on their backs from being whipped. Additionally, they cannot find a comfortable position because their feet are bound in stocks.

Yet, despite their circumstances, they are determined to praise God. They know the deep, inner joy of obeying and serving Him, of knowing He is on their side. Perhaps feebly, they begin to sing. Strengthened by the Holy Spirit and the edification of the words of their song, their hearts are encouraged.

Thus, in the darkest hour of their lives at this point, Paul and Silas are demonstrating a living testimony to the other prisoners, and ultimately, to the jailer and his household.

It was not the music, but their faith in God through their trial that drew others to Christ.

And so it should be in our lives as believers who claim the name of Jesus Christ as our Lord and Savior.

14. *It's the worship leader's responsibility to lead the congregation into worship (or teach them how to worship).*

True worship comes from people's hearts, and a worship leader cannot change the people's hearts, no matter how upbeat the music. But with CCM, the congregation's heart is in the excitement of the carnal music, rather than personal worship. (Take the music away and the point will be proven.)

Remember the old saying, "You can lead a horse to water, but you can't make him drink"? Similarly, a worship leader may be leading the music, but he can't make a person worship. Furthermore, CCM grieves discerning Christians so that they are *unable* to worship.

The terms "praise" and "worship" in our day have been used interchangeably, however, they are not always the same thing. We praise God for Who He is—for His attributes—and this can lead to worship. When we worship, we increasingly become aware of how sinful we are and how holy God is, and, this in turn, can also lead to praise. It is this blending of meanings that I will use when discussing worship in this section.

True worship comes from a person's heart. While a worship leader may be able to motivate people *outwardly*, through providing upbeat music, *a worship leader is powerless to change people's hearts.* And by using carnal music to get everyone "excited" about the Lord, the worship leader is, in reality, unknowingly manipulating people into believing that they've experienced worship.

This artificially induced worship is robbing God of the true worship He deserves, and at the same time, is robbing believers of true worship that should come from within themselves. A believer who is worshipping from his or her heart won't need a worship leader to lead him into worship; nor will he need music as an aid in order to experience worship.

But a worship experience which has been contrived for people actually masks their true relationship to God and is only temporary, necessitating their participation in an upbeat worship service week after week so that they can have an experience that leads them to believe they're worshipping God—so that they can be emotionally satisfied.

The worship leader is not a cheerleader for God, nor is he or she an emcee for a slick and seamless musical production, which easily becomes a show and contrives to initiate what is lacking spiritually. Worship leaders need to first experience worship in their own lives on a daily basis, without music. Then they will be able to exhibit an example of true worship, not only in congregational worship, but as a living example to others of a personal, vibrant relationship to God.

The responsibility of the worship leader should be to provide a pure and righteous musical opportunity for the congregation to truly hear from the Lord, rather than externally motivating the people to get excited about Jesus by using musical techniques that appeal to their flesh. For only then will a worship leader be able to stand before God with a clear conscience that he or she did not inadvertently manipulate people into thinking they were worshipping God, when in fact they weren't.

Perhaps we need to go back to the earlier titles of song leader, or music minister, as these convey the truer function of the person who helps the congregation and instrumentalists stay musically together during a song.

And let people be convicted that if they are not experiencing worship *from within themselves*—without upbeat music—there is something wrong with their relationship to God.

15. *People aren't going to listen to "churchy" music anymore—it's boring. We have to use music that will draw*

people to our churches; CCM meets that criteria, because it's similar to the music they listen to everyday.

Enticing people to come to our churches by offering sensual, flesh-pleasing rock music that has been labeled "Christian" is a misrepresentation of Holy God and shows that our faith is in our music, not in God's ability to draw people to Himself.

To better understand how good music does not necessarily repel, or put people off, let's consider the movie industry.

Attending movies is a major leisure time activity of many youth and young adults. Many times, people are exposed to good music, music that follows biblical principles, during a movie. Do they avoid the cinema because of this? No.

People go to the movies for the story line; music is secondary. Movies don't have to have upbeat music in order to draw people, and neither should our churches.

Of course, entertainment is the draw for the motion picture industry. The entertainment factor is a key ingredient to drawing people to any event. And by using upbeat music in order to draw people to our churches, we've now provided entertainment, and the spoken Word of God is secondary. Therefore, the draw of CCM is entertainment rather than true worship.

You don't believe this? Then why do some people leave after the song service, just before the preaching? (Yes, it happens.)

Each generation thinks it is moving closer to God, when in fact they are moving away. Why else is it that many churches now have to rely on programs, exciting music, plays, bands, and special events in order to keep people in the pews?

If we announced a simple prayer meeting with no bells or whistles, how many people would come? Not many, because there's no entertainment value in a prayer meeting.

The notion that we have to please the people in order to get their attention is a false idea, anyway. The gospel message is not about pleasing or entertaining people. It is about showing people that they're sinners, in need of a Savior—Jesus Christ. I can think of no one who wants to be told that he or she is a sinner with a capital "S," can you?

The natural person (in his or her sinful, unregenerate state) doesn't truly seek God, pure and simple. The Bible plainly tells us this.[18] But people will do a few noble things to get on God's "good side."

People will go to church to assuage their conscience, but at least with CCM they can enjoy it. The preaching is something they endure, something they put up with, so that they can be entertained by the music. And because they are in church, they've done their duty for God. So, if the musical style is familiar to the unregenerate person, it is actually a comfort because it is non-convicting. Yes, the lyrics may provide some emotional impact, may impart some spiritual truth, but the musical style of CCM itself is non-convicting. It candy-coats the message of the lyrics because it is exactly the kind of musical message people want to hear. Therefore, the true impact of the lyrics is diluted.

Traditionally played hymns, on the other hand, *are* convicting—both lyrically and musically. To a true believer, they are edifying, refreshing, full of doctrine, and a comfort to our battle-weary souls. To the non-believer or those who subscribe to CCM, the traditional style is boring.

Could it be that the word *boring* is really a substitute for the word *convicting*?

For example, if we were to take most CCM and remove the words, it would be accepted in any bar or nightclub. Nothing very convicting in that, is there?

Go to those same nightclubs and play traditional hymns with no lyrics. They would throw us out. Why? They know that this style of music does not belong in a nightclub. The customers would leave because they would be uncomfortable—*they would be convicted.* But they don't want to be convicted; they want their lifestyles to be validated, and, musically, CCM also provides a type of validation, an excuse for our present lifestyle.

We live in a time in which people seek to occupy themselves through busyness and entertainment. Very few people carve out true down time—no television or radio, no activities or sports—we keep busy, busy, busy. If we truly wanted to be still before the Lord, we could find the time; after all, we find time to read the newspaper, look at magazines, read books, or enjoy a hobby.

The purpose for all this busyness, whether or not we like to admit it, is to run away from God. We don't want to be still before God and hear from Him because we're afraid of being convicted, afraid of being still long enough to truly contemplate our sinfulness and responsibility before God. And CCM contributes to this running away because it is providing musical busyness, whereby we can feel like we've worshipped God and have been to church, but in reality we've been entertained. Our carnal music preference has been validated, and once again, we have done our duty, without really having seen ourselves as God wants us to see ourselves.

So when we hear traditional hymns, we say they are boring. But the problem is not with the hymns; the problem lies within ourselves because we seek to be entertained.

Our churches should not exist to provide entertainment week after week so that people will come through the doors. They should exist solely to exalt God by providing biblically-oriented help for His followers as they seek to be like Christ, serve others, and worship Him.

Therefore, music that represents God *should* be different. Not only in lyrics, but in style. Just as the true gospel should demonstrate the righteousness of God, so should our Christian music, which represents Him, be righteous in every way; the result of which will be convicting to the unbeliever, while at the same time be comforting to the believer. People must be convicted on every level because they cannot be saved without true conviction of their sins in the first place.[19]

So, no, many people won't listen to "churchy" music unless they are truly drawn to God and mean business. Enticing them with an entertaining musical style they are comfortable with is dishonest because sensual (carnal) music techniques do not represent a holy God. Let's take the music away, and see who *does* mean business!

God already knows.

16. *But traditional hymns really are boring.*

Only because we have created in ourselves an appetite for upbeat music.

I agree that some hymns can be dragged along far too slowly, and there's certainly no demonstration of joy in the Lord when this happens. We should not equate "spiritual" with dull and slow music. Neither should we equate "revival" with upbeat rock music that feeds our flesh. But the truth is that because we've become so accustomed to upbeat music, we no longer accept music which doesn't "tickle our ears." Our preference has changed.

Any desire—good or bad—can be fed so that we want more and more of whatever we are constantly thinking about or listening to. For example: We want (desire) more money, a bigger or nicer house, nicer clothes, a leaner or better body, success, recognition, and, of course, many sensual sins, etc. (Hopefully, we desire godliness in our lives.) And as we feed those desires by continually thinking about them, we find ourselves increasingly desiring the object of our thoughts—rightly or wrongly.

But instead of feeding a wrong desire, in this case, listening to carnal music, we need to reprogram our thinking, as well as make a conscious decision to say no to our desire for music that appeals to our flesh.

This is a biblical concept, which is commonly referred to as "denial of self." Jesus says, "If any man will come after me, *let him deny himself*, and take up his cross, and follow me" (Matt. 16:24, emphasis mine).

Even more strongly, Paul tells us in Titus 2:12 that God's grace, in bringing salvation, "[teaches] us that, *denying ungodliness and worldly lusts*, we should live soberly, righteously, and godly, in this present world" (emphasis mine).

Unfortunately, denial of our carnal, fleshly self is a foreign concept to many twenty-first century Christians in America.

Biblical self-denial is not to be confused with those who practice self-denial in order to obtain their own brand of righteousness, i.e., denying themselves of a certain activity or food for a length of time in order to merit God's favor.

Biblical self-denial is *making a conscious decision* to not give in to a particular sinful habit, so that Jesus' righteousness, through the Holy Spirit, may be worked out in us. In regard to music, we should be making a conscious decision to avoid any music (including CCM) that appeals to our carnal self, and then replace that music with God-honoring music, such as traditional hymns and other music that would please God.[D]

Finally, if our hearts truly desire to please Him in every way, if we have a close relationship to Him apart from music, those hymns won't be so boring anymore.

Preferences *can* change.

17. *Then how do we get people to come to our churches?*

Prayer, along with godly living by following the two Great Commandments, will create a thirst in others to have the peace of God for themselves.

Which takes more faith—programs, activities, and exciting music, or prayer? With prayer, we know that it is God moving, and that it was nothing we did ourselves. Seeing Him move in this way is invigorating for the life of a church and increases our faith. And He gets the glory instead of our "proven" methods. (Be honest, haven't we been guilty of saying it's the music [a method] that gets people to come to the church?)

Furthermore, as we live out our lives in obedience to God, by loving Him and loving others, people will see that there is something to Christianity; that there is something of real substance, and they will want it for themselves. I believe that when Jesus said we are the "salt of the earth,"[20] part of what He was referring to is that just as eating salt creates a thirst, lives lived for Him will create a "thirst" in unbelievers, and they will want what we have as Christians. But if our lives are so much like theirs anyway, if our music is exactly the same as theirs only with "better" lyrics, they won't really understand what being a true Christian is because we won't have demonstrated an obedient and godly life.

While I disagree with the CCM method of reaching the seemingly unreachable, e.g., teens going through tough times, we should at least commend those who are trying to love these youth where they're at by reaching out to them. I think many people in the Church are guilty of not accepting certain types of groups. Nevertheless, when we witness, we must all be very careful that we are not actually witnessing in a way that misrepresents Jesus, so that people are accepting our "method," rather than truly accepting Christ as their Savior. If we remove the CCM and they fall away, they *have* accepted the method—not Jesus—and we will be accountable.

Certainly, we should help meet the needs of people in our communities, pass out gospel literature, have fellowships, Bible studies, and occasional special programs. But we should never compromise God's standards in any of these.

Too often, though, we plan activities, then ask God to bless our efforts, instead of first asking God which activities, if any, we should pursue. We like to see instant results and numbers; God wants to see our faith. (Read Hebrews 11.)

Nevertheless, we are guilty of having placed our faith in our methods, rather than placing our faith and trust in God.

18. *If it weren't for "accidentally" hearing CCM on the radio, I wouldn't be in a Bible study and church today.*

This statement shows more faith in the CCM than in God's power to draw people to Himself. A person can't say that CCM is *the* reason he or she has turned to God, because God is sovereign.

As discussed in the first example about salvation at concerts, God can and does use anything to get our attention. How do we know that God could not have just as well used something else at that particular time in our life? How do we know that we did or did not have an "appointment" with God? We can't know.

God is sovereign. There are amazing stories about people in remote countries just waiting for someone to bring them information about the true God.[21] And what about the multitudes of testimonies of how a simple Gideon Bible placed in a hotel room resulted in the salvation and changed life of someone in a desperate circumstance? *God* is in the business of drawing people to Himself. He doesn't need CCM—or any other method we may contrive—to get people's attention. In no way are *we* able to get people into the kingdom without the power of God's Holy Spirit.

When God draws someone, He will do it by using whatever circumstance a person is in at the moment. This does not necessarily validate the circumstance. Through the Holy Spirit, God draws, convicts, and woos us wherever we are. He takes us from where we are, but He doesn't leave us there.

We should only rejoice in the fact that God, through whatever means, caused us to turn to Him.

19. *I would not have considered being a Christian if it weren't for CCM. CCM has done a lot of good.*

How do you know for sure? Would you still follow Jesus if the music was taken away?

This is similar to the previous statement, as well as several others yet to be discussed, that disallow for God's sovereignty in a person's salvation or recommitment to Jesus Christ. Recall Paul's statement in 1 Corinthians 3:6–7: "I planted, Apollos watered, but *God* gave the increase. So then neither he who plants is anything, nor he who waters, but *God* who gives the increase" (NKJV, emphasis mine).

It is *only* God Who should get the credit, not man, nor any method man uses, including CCM. Therefore we cannot credit CCM as having done "a lot of good." Especially so because of contemporary Christian music's appeal to the flesh, which is contrary to Scripture's teaching about denying our flesh.[22]

I will acknowledge that some CCM lyrics may have truly met people's spiritual needs and given them something worthwhile to consider, ultimately leading them to the Lord Jesus Christ, yet the same could be said of some secular music, as well. It is God Who draws people to Himself, and it is God Who "gives the increase," and *He* may use whatever means to that end. *We* may not.

Many people, however, are crediting CCM and its various musical styles with the ability to draw people to Christ and change lives. But if we remove these styles of music, will people continue to follow Jesus? If not, where is their faith—in CCM, or in the Lord Jesus?

And would you be willing to test your relationship to Him by removing CCM from your life? If not, why not?

20. *I'd rather my teenagers go to a CCM concert than to a secular rock concert.*

The same things that go on at secular rock concerts go on at many CCM concerts.[23]

In St. Louis, a young teenage girl was recently interviewed on the radio about why she liked a certain secular performer who had just given a concert. She said, "I liked the way his hips moved."

Parents, we are just deceiving ourselves to think that our kids who attend CCM concerts react any differently.

Even if entire families go together, it's a matter of the parents moving down to the kids' level of standards, rather than the parents training the kids up to God's standards through providing a godly example of discernment and wisdom by their choice of righteous entertainment.

There are other wholesome alternatives for our children's entertainment. What did the Christian youth do before CCM?

21. *I'd rather my kids listen to CCM than to secular rock music, and at least they're going to church now.*

If there were no CCM, would your kids still follow Jesus? (Ask them to prove it.)

I can certainly understand the supposition that CCM is a better alternative than secular rock music, in light of the filth that secular rock music portrays through videos and lyrics. Yet, if the truth were known, many Christian teens are listening to secular rock as well as CCM, and not only that, they are also viewing MTV. In fact, at least one Christian organization that I know of actually OK's some secular pop/rock music! And because we have embraced CCM, we have lost our discernment, accepted some secular rock as OK, and the lines between the world and the Church have become blurred; there is no real distinction anymore. This would not have been true forty years ago.

To make our case for contemporary Christian music (as well as some secular rock music) in the Christian youth culture, we reason that our kids can listen to it and maintain their values as Christians, yet still fit in to the mainstream of teenage attitudes and culture. And we reason (subconsciously or consciously) that they can have the best of both worlds, actually, since this is such a "difficult" time of life for them anyway.

This is dangerous reasoning because *what we've actually done is "sold out" our youth to a compromised lifestyle, if they are really saved at all.*

Instead of giving them valuable tools and meaningful instruction from God's Word, we've encouraged them in carnal Christianity that seeks to feed the flesh, rather than having taught them to deny their flesh and feed their spirits. And, as mentioned before, denial of the flesh is a concept that is essential if we are to become increasingly holy in our daily lives, if we're to be of any real worth to the kingdom of God.

Additionally, we've basically allowed the teen culture to dictate to us what they will listen to. The attitude is, "If you want to reach me, you're going to have to play the music I want to hear." This puts a condition on their salvation, and allowing this attitude promotes further rebellion and a spirit of independence instead of biblical submission to God's ways, which is what God greatly desires for *every one* of His children.

We need to also realize that as we put our blessing on CCM, we are actually encouraging and feeding the teens vs. adults conflict, which began around the time of the advent of rock music many years ago, and we are giving them what they already have in the secular world. Do we really want our children to be "harlots-in-training" as they listen to and imitate the sensuality found in most CCM? How will this meet their spiritual needs? *Nowhere* in the Bible does it tell us that teens are allowed to behave any differently than any other believer.

Ecclesiastes 11:9–10 tells the youth that they *will* be judged for their actions. Do we, as parents (or youth leaders) want our children to be judged for behavior we encouraged which is contrary to Scripture? Verse 10 directly instructs them to, ". . . put away evil from thy flesh. . . ." And we have seen that most CCM *does* appeal to the carnal self—the flesh.

Jesus requires the same of all who come to Him.[24] Some things in life we have to do whether or not we like them. This is just a fact of life, true for both teens and adults.

In past generations, the family went to church and there was no question of, "What does this church offer me or my family?" Or, "Do my children/teens like the music?" People went to church because it was the right thing to do, to worship God and learn about Him.

But this generation seeks to please itself. Even as Christians, most of us have lost the concept of duty and obligation and instead are emotionally driven.

Ask your teenager: "If there were no CCM, would you still follow Jesus?" And, if he or she says, yes, challenge them to prove it by removing it from their life.

This is entirely biblical, for what Paul admonished the Corinthians applies to us, as well: "Examine yourselves, whether ye be in the faith; prove your own selves . . ." (2 Cor. 13:5a).[25]

22. *How do we reach teenagers?*

Isn't God powerful enough that He can reach our teenagers without CCM?

How were teens saved *before* CCM? The same way God has outlined in Scripture for *everyone*—through the preaching of the Word: ". . . faith cometh by hearing, and hearing by the word of God" (Rom. 10:17). And Christians—even teens—who share their testimonies and live out changed lives send a powerful message, also. Just like everyone else, teens must be truly convicted that they are sinners in need of a Savior so that they will turn to Jesus out of desperation, a requirement for anyone who desires true salvation.

Parents, where is *our* faith? Settling for a compromise in CCM is not a demonstration of our faith in God. While the lyrics are moral—and may be even biblical—CCM doesn't save our kids. What its underlying musical message does do is encourage them in worldly attitudes and behaviors that are contrary to Scripture.

Is this what you really want for your children?[E] Will they thank you in years to come for the lower standards you allowed in their Christian life? Which teachers in your own life do you have respect for now as an adult: those who let the kids run over them, or those who had high expectations? And what is God's standard for all of His children?

23. *I've seen changed lives from CCM.*

People can be motivated to change through many of life's circumstances—with or without the Holy Spirit. Their "change" doesn't necessarily vindicate the event.

I will not question the work of the Holy Spirit through whatever avenue He seeks to move. Yet we need to be aware that people, *of their own volition,* can also make their lives better, perhaps having been inspired through any one of a variety of circumstances or ideas.

Because this statement is so similar to the first statement, however ("People are saved at CCM concerts"), there's no need to discuss this further.

24. I feel "called" to this ministry.

While a person may be called to a ministry through music, God never calls people to "unrighteousness" in any ministry—unrighteousness demonstrated through loose vocals and carnal music techniques.

There's no doubt that there are many talented Christian musicians, composers, and vocalists in the world. And because CCM is so widespread and has the blessing of the majority of Christians, it would be easy to believe that one was called to minister with CCM.

But because of this widespread belief that CCM is OK, we are actually justifying each other's practice of using carnal music for both our personal listening and for the service of the Lord.

We must be very careful when we say we are called to do something for the Lord, because our own feelings and ambitions can get in the way of hearing clearly from Him.

And it's also possible for us to get a calling half right, meaning, yes, we are called, but no, not to those methods (meaning CCM).

Seemingly miraculous circumstances and other people's opinions about a felt calling do not necessarily mean God is working or confirming our decision. Satan is very good at creating circumstances also, and every one of us has an opinion on most everything, whether or not our opinion is biblical.

What does God's Word say about our calling to service for Him?

Ephesians 4:1: "I . . . beseech you to walk worthy of the calling with which you were called."

1 Thessalonians 4:7: "For God did not call us to uncleanness, but in holiness."

And, 1 Peter 1:15–16: ". . . but as He who called you is holy, you also be holy in all your conduct, because it is written, 'Be holy, for I am holy.'" (All taken from NKJV.)

Notice the words *worthy, holiness,* and *holy.* Can we rightly apply these words to any music (CCM included) that employs specific, *identifiable* methods that can—and do—cause a carnal response in the listener? I seriously doubt it.

And while God does call people to minister with music, would God ever call anyone to use readily identifiable, sensual music techniques in order to share His message? Would He ever ask us to violate scriptural principles in order to minister for Him? Would He ever lead us into unrighteousness?

The answer to each of these questions has to be a resounding, "No."

25. God gave me my talent.

There are also numerous secular musicians, composers, and vocalists who have, undeniably, amazing raw talent.

As Christians, though, it is our responsibility to channel our talents according to scriptural principles—not according to worldly methods or ideals. In fact, following scriptural principles provides music that far surpasses what is offered by the world. For example, J.S. Bach was a brilliant (Christian) composer of his time, and to this day his music continues to be studied and respected for its depth, complexity, and sheer genius by both secular and nonsecular musicians. Composing both secular and sacred music, Bach never compromised his Christian faith, but held firmly to the belief that music's main objective should be for the glory of God.

Likewise, *we* cannot excuse our talent to be used for any means other than those that follow biblical principles, and those principles do not allow for the use of sensual techniques in music, Christian or otherwise.

26. *I know people who are true Christians who sing CCM and their hearts are "right."*

If we truly love God as we say we do, we'll want to please Him with music that does not contain sensual techniques in any way, shape or form—lyrically, vocally, or musically.

According to God's Word, we cannot even know our own hearts, let alone another person's: "The heart is deceitful above all things, and desperately wicked: who can know it?" (Jeremiah 17:9).

If a woman states, "I can wear any kind of clothing I want, even if it's revealing; God knows my heart," we would seriously question her desire to please God, wouldn't we? As a person matures in the Lord, as He molds and shapes our hearts, the evidence of this will show up externally. But just because a person claims his or her heart is right, doesn't necessarily mean he or she is in one accord with God's thinking on any issue.

While this clothing example may be obvious to us, the use of CCM by Christians whose heart *is* right is not so obvious. The reason is because CCM is a mixture of truth and error.

Truth, in that the lyrics can be very meaningful, even fully scriptural. Error, in that the musical vehicle makes use of sensual techniques to which we have become so accustomed, desensitized, and numbed.

If our heart's desire is to truly please God, then we have to consider what is pleasing to Him. Are identifiable, sensual techniques in our Christian music pleasing to Him when we know that other forms of overt sensuality are wrong? I don't think we can honestly say that they are.

So even if a Christian's overall heart is right (in our eyes), *our heart condition alone does not make our choices valid in the sight of God.* We must follow through with biblically-sound choices, which are the only choices that are legitimate to God. As James 2:20 tells us, ". . . faith without works is dead."

27. *The motivation (intention) of the performer/composer, conveyed through the lyrics, is all that matters.*

New Age music, rock music, and even movie soundtrack music, each have a musical mood they want to convey to the listener independent of, or even in absence of, lyrics. The songwriters/composers do this through specific musical techniques.

I covered this somewhat in my first book, but this needs further discussion. To understand how motivation and music are intertwined, let's look at New Age music.

Have you ever listened to New Age music? It's very relaxing and peaceful, isn't it?

New Age music's motivation (goal) is to relax the listener, calm the mind, and, ultimately, open the mind to demonic powers.[26] *This is accomplished through specific musical techniques.*

Similarly, secular rock music's goal has been admittedly to cause the listener to lose his or her inhibitions and react with sensual body movements.[27] Again, this is accomplished through specific musical techniques, apart from the lyrics.[F]

And what about movie soundtracks? These, too, create and set the mood for any given part of a movie—all by using specific musical techniques.

In all of these examples, it is not enough for the composers to simply say that their motivation is to accomplish these specific goals and then use any music they like. To the contrary, they know for a certainty that specific techniques and musical styles must be used in order to produce a specific reaction they are wanting the listener to experience; they know that specific musical techniques must be used in order to send a specific message or set a particular mood.

Understanding this concept, that the use of specific musical techniques are necessary to accomplish specific goals, helps us to realize that the use of rock music techniques that have been designed to appeal to our carnal self cannot be "borrowed" for use in Christian music.

What is the message we want God to hear musically when we worship Him? What is the message we want other Christians to hear? And what is the message we want to convey to non-believers? What reaction in each of these instances do we want the listener to experience?

To every one of these listeners we are communicating a message through the music itself, not only through the lyrics. And by using sensual, flesh-pleasing musical techniques and vocal inflections, we are communicating to our listener—God—that we are a sensual, flesh-pleasing people, regardless of what our mouths are saying, regardless of what we think our heart motivation truly is.

Because we do have a choice of musical techniques and the knowledge of how to apply them, we can very well match our motivational goals of worship, edification, and evangelism with proper musical techniques that will honestly please God and demonstrate to Him that we are set apart believers intent on living out holy lives.[28]

Additionally, by using righteous techniques in our music, the message our Christian music will send to unbelievers is one of purity, and ultimately, *conviction* in their lives, which is essential for true repentance and salvation.

Therefore, our motivation, or desire, to minister through CCM cannot truly be the sole consideration for our music, because to use identifiable musical techniques that appeal to the flesh of man is not only contrary to the Word of God, but is also contrary to our goals for worship and evangelism. Goals which should be to honor God in His holiness, encourage believers toward righteousness, strengthen them in their walk with the Lord, and convict unbelievers of their sins.

We've got to realize that no matter what the motivation of the band/performer is, people are still reacting to the carnal music in a carnal manner, regardless of what the lyrics communicate. If, as many claim, the words are more important (carry more weight) than the music, then why do secular artists choose a rock or jazz style of music to convey their lurid lyrics rather than a hymn-like tune? Wouldn't the lyrical content be the same? Do you see how this does not work? Secular artists understand far better than most Christians that the musical style they choose as a vehicle for their lyrics *is* important.

But by using the exact same identifiable techniques that secular rock music artists have devised to appeal sensually to their audiences, CCM has sent the wrong musical message to its listeners, although the motivation—and even the lyrics—may have been initially right.

God has told us quite frankly in 1 Samuel 15:22: ". . . Behold, to obey is better than sacrifice, and to hearken than the fat of rams."

In other words, as this is applied to Christian music, our obedience to His Word is far more important to Him than any offering in song which doesn't follow biblical righteousness in the musical style—no matter how sincere we may be.

28. *It's all relative; everyone has his or her own tastes.*

There are specific musical techniques that can be objectively identified as having been designed to appeal to our carnal self.

The argument here is that any and all music is only subjective, not objective. Or, to clarify, we say that musical styles are a matter of personal preference (subjective); there are no concrete (objective) methods that can be used to judge it.

To a small degree this is true, but the exercise of personal taste for the believer is really only valid within the parameters God has outlined in His Word. Unfortunately, we would prefer to say that all music is a matter of subjectiveness (personal opinion), rather than submit to God and learn and exercise true musical discernment. And when we say that our musical choices are a matter of opinion/preference, we put ourselves as the authority rather than God.

As we have seen, however, we can prove that there are specific musical techniques that cause our bodies to react in impure movements, as well as appeal to our flesh in other ways. These techniques can be objectively identified.[G] (Remember, we're talking about techniques that call forth from our bodies a desire to move in ways that are sensual, or that employ other very subtle sensual techniques; we are not talking about those musical techniques that stimulate our intellect—four-part harmony, or the counterpoint music of Bach, for instance.)

Yet once we move into the boundaries God has given us, "spiritual (non-carnal) songs," we are free to exercise our personal preferences, in both sacred and secular music.

For example, you may like Gregorian chant; I may not. We can both like the Baroque style. One of us may also like some Romantic period composers, but dislike others. Or Austrian folk music may be one of your favorite styles of music.

Each of these styles of music follows biblical principles, and so within the realm of biblically acceptable music, there can be many individual preferences. Amazingly, the list of music that complies with biblical principles is extensive.[H]

But our evaluation of music does not end at the church door. As Christians, we should evaluate *all* music according to biblical principles—removing any music from our lives that is not pleasing to God, either through its lyrics or through its style. No longer should our music be a matter of taste or opinion, it becomes a matter of discernment, obedience, and holiness, as we work out our personal sanctification. I know from experience that changing musical preference is not easy, but it is possible.

Have *you* surrendered to Him in this area? Have you asked Him to change your heart? And are you willing to deny your personal preference in order to obey Him?

If not, why not?

29. *Don't put God in a box.*

This statement attempts to shift the focus onto God, rather than take responsibility for the sensual techniques used in Christian music.

The "in a box" excuse suggests that we shouldn't limit God by saying that He *only* works through certain methods, i.e. hymns. Once again, I'm not implying this at all, as indicated in my response to the first statement about salvation at CCM concerts. No one could put God in a box, anyway. Yet He has placed limitations on Himself: He will not lie, nor will He change.[29]

We, as Christians, also need to limit certain behavior in our lives, even to the point of some of those behaviors being totally removed.

But we don't like to talk about self-imposed limitations in our own lives, especially if it's something we don't want to give up: in this case, CCM. God, however, has told us in His Word that limiting ourselves for the gospel's sake *is* essential for godly living.

Titus 2:11–12 puts it this way: "For the grace of God that brings salvation has appeared to all men, teaching us that, denying ungodliness and worldly lusts, we should live soberly, righteously, and godly in the present age" (NKJV).[30] This applies to all areas of our lives that should be under His authority—including our music.

Concerning CCM, the "in a box" statement is actually avoiding our own personal responsibility to limit ourselves as we should, by representing God through music that does not utilize sensual techniques (i.e., "ungodliness and worldly lusts"), and we use this phrase in an attempt to shift the focus onto Him so that we may continue to excuse our sensual music practices.

But where in the Bible does it say, "anything goes," in order to reach the lost? Are God's requirements for holiness among His people suspended when we evangelize?

30. We must be "all things to all men" as Paul said.

Paul would have stopped short at crossing the line to appeal to people's flesh. As CCM musicians and vocalists "become all things to all people," however, in essence, they are really becoming sensual, carnal, and worldly in their presentation of Christian music.

Taken from 1 Corinthians 9:22: ". . . I am made all things to all men, that I might by all means save some," this defense sounds good, even spiritual. Nevertheless, this reasoning has not been sufficiently and logically thought through.

In the context of this passage, as well as in Paul's entire Christian life, this argument does not hold water. We need to back up to verse 20 to see the intended meaning. Paul is talking about being *culturally* as the people he was trying to reach (by following the Jewish customs with the Jewish people, or eating as the Gentiles ate), so that they could better listen. Nothing more. Paul would have *never* crossed the line to appeal to people's carnal, fleshly tendencies. He simply adopted certain lifestyle customs so that unbelievers would not be offended, then he could gain their trust and preach about Jesus Christ.

This is just basic missionary wisdom. For example, some missionaries dress similarly to the culture they are living in (and as modesty dictates) so that they are better accepted into that culture and may then share the gospel.

Similarly, if you or I were to go to a culture that believed that the color red was evil, we would be foolish to wear or use red in any form, because no matter what we did, no matter how spiritual we were, the people couldn't "hear" our message and the gospel would be hindered.

We should fit in and honor basic cultural habits so that people are open to what we have to share. But *never* are we to cross the line into sin. God never asks that of us, and indeed, warns us against committing sin. He will honor our stand for righteousness, and we will gain the respect of unbelievers.

As Americans, however, we already fit in our culture, and can easily move within the subcultures with minor adjustments and/or prior experience because we might have come out of a certain lifestyle. Certainly ex-drug-addicts minister to other drug-addicts more believably than someone who has never taken a single street drug. But the ex-drug addict would not return to that lifestyle just to be "all things to all men."

This concept applies to all layers of (American) life. I don't have to have multiple body piercings to talk to the young woman at the discount store about the Lord Jesus Christ. She accepts me, and I accept her. We already have the common American experience, especially so because of the media that permeates our society, detailing people's lives more than we care to know.

But as we evaluate contemporary Christian music as being "all things to all men," we see that it has actually imitated symbols of rebellion and carnality in America under the banner of evangelism.

We have crossed the line into sin.

Yes, this is a very strong statement, yet most people are simply not making the connection between the fact that these rock music techniques appeal to the flesh, and to purposely use them in Christian music *is* sin—regardless of our motives (see number 27).

Consider what God's Word plainly tells us: "All unrighteousness is sin . . ." (1 John 5:17).

Is it righteous that through CCM we are appealing to the baser, carnal desires of man by the use of secular rock music techniques, both vocally and instrumentally? Is it righteous that this music encourages people, Christians and non-Christians alike, to yield their bodies to certain suggestive movements as "servants to uncleanness" as opposed to yielding their bodies "servants to righteousness unto holiness"?[31]

Anyone would be hard-pressed to answer to God that these practices are, indeed, righteous.

We have to realize as Christians that we cannot realistically be all things to all people. We cannot and should not please all people, especially when sin is involved, and we're *not* going to be liked and approved of by the world if we are true Christians.

Yes, CCM is all things to all people; it pleases the masses. There are styles for every taste, it encourages (sinful) carnal dancing and chaos at some concerts. It even gets awards in both worlds—secular and nonsecular.

In contrast, Paul was beaten, whipped, imprisoned, stoned, left for dead, and went without food.[32] From this we may conclude that he was *not* "all things to all men" of his time. Furthermore, he succinctly tells us in Galatians

1:10, "For do I now persuade men, or God? or do I seek to please men? for if I yet pleased men, I should not be the servant of Christ."

So was Paul all things to all men in every sense of our modern-day application concerning CCM? Not at all. Paul understood that to be all things to all men did not mean to encourage any of their present sin, nor to imitate it. He understood that within each culture there was a line he must not cross. In fact, he further tells us in the same passage of 1 Corinthians 9, verse 27, ". . . I discipline my body and bring it into subjection, lest, when I have preached to others, I myself should become disqualified" (NKJV).

Paul was above reproach.

31. The Bible (New Testament) teaches "everything in moderation."

We are not to sin, even in moderation. And because CCM uses techniques that appeal to our carnal self, with the ability to cause impure and ungodly movements in its listeners, CCM not only causes us to sin, it is sinful in and of itself.

There is no single Scripture from which we can draw the phrase everything-in-moderation statement,[1] although it may be concluded that there are certain things in life that allow for moderation.

For example, moderate (without excess) food intake. And while I would contend that any alcohol consumption is a bad testimony for a changed life through Jesus Christ, some would argue that it is not expressly forbidden in Scripture, therefore moderation applies to that, as well. Additionally, the term *self-control* may be included as we define biblical moderation, and self-control is very essential to victorious Christian living.

In all things, however, we are to be acutely aware of the testimony we are living before other people—believers and unbelievers alike—ultimately answering to God for our actions.

While the statement "everything in moderation" sounds reasonable, we need to think this through to its logical conclusion. Namely, are we allowed moderation in sin? Absolutely not.

Hopefully by now you will have seen the link between sin and the purposeful use of sensual music techniques in contemporary Christian music. Therefore, to continue to use such techniques in our music is not simply a matter of allowing everything in moderation.

Because once we're aware there's a problem with certain musical techniques, as with any other lifestyle choice in which we know better, it then becomes a matter of *choosing* to sin.

32. The Bible says, "Let every man be fully persuaded in his own mind."

Many people are fully persuaded about innumerable ideas that are totally unbiblical. Our personal belief about any issue doesn't necessarily make our belief biblical.

Taken from Romans 14:5, this argument asserts that whatever one chooses to believe (about music) is all that matters as long as he or she is sincere in their devotion to God and as long as his or her belief is not expressly forbidden in Scripture. Let each of us be fully persuaded, and we may agree to disagree.

Concerning CCM, this argument is invalid for several reasons.

First, it places our own thinking (our own beliefs) above the whole counsel of Scripture regarding the issue of Christian music.

Second, it disallows for the fact that many people are fully persuaded about a myriad of ideas that are totally unbiblical.

For example, there are people who are fully persuaded that works gain God's approval, and, therefore, our salvation. There are people who are fully persuaded that there is no Trinity. There are people who are fully persuaded that there is no real hell.

And which of these is the correct viewpoint, pre-tribulation or post-tribulation rapture? Or maybe it's mid-tribulation rapture!

So you see, just because we are fully persuaded (in our own mind) about something, our personal persuasion doesn't necessarily make our belief doctrinally sound.

Last, and perhaps most important, the independent use of this Scripture ignores the entire context of the passage, which is speaking about side issues in our lives, such as eating or abstaining from certain food. Issues which have no influence on a life that seeks after righteousness. Issues that do not necessarily make us more Christlike (e.g., the kind of car we drive, our choice of furniture, what colors we choose for our clothing, etc.)

This passage simply guides us to be sensitive to our conscience, and, therefore, the Holy Spirit, in the side issues of our lives, remembering that He will *never* lead us contrary to scriptural principles.

But the use of sinful musical practices, either in secular or sacred music, do have relevance in the life of a Christian who truly seeks after righteousness. We cannot claim that we are fully persuaded that CCM is acceptable in our own life, or that CCM is a side issue of no real importance, when it can be easily proven at most any concert that CCM promotes ungodly behavior in our carnal self, rather than Christ-like behaviors of self-control and righteousness.

So unlike our choice of a particular food, which won't affect our personal sanctification either positively or negatively, our choice of music does influence our Christian witness and our personal walk with Jesus Christ.

But in reality, we don't want to be fully persuaded that CCM is unbiblical, because we like it too much and are unwilling to give it up.

33. ". . . *there is nothing unclean of itself: but to him that esteemeth any thing to be unclean, to him it is unclean"* (Rom. 14:14).

This Scripture passage also refers to the side issues in life that have no impact on our personal sanctification. CCM, because of its carnal appeal, *does* have an impact and leads us away from personal holiness. Therefore, this passage cannot be applied to CCM.

The argument here is that we are able to determine for ourselves which musical practices are acceptable in our own lives, and everyone is allowed to have a different viewpoint. And just because CCM is wrong for one person, doesn't make it wrong for another person.

This Scripture from Romans is found in the middle of a passage that explains about our freedom from the Old

Testament food restrictions, and also provides us with the broader application that we are to be careful not to exercise our liberty in Christ to such an extent as to make a fellow Christian stumble, or make a non-believer blaspheme God. (See Rom. 14:14–23.)

To help us to better understand how this may be applied to music in general, and CCM in particular, my pastor's wife has made the following observations: If a person who couldn't speak our language attended a CCM concert, yet saw the audience dancing and carrying on exactly like audiences behave at secular concerts, what would that person's conclusion be? What would he or she conclude if a comparison were made between the music at your church and the rock music of secular society? Would God be honored? Would the person be drawn to God "without a word"? Would he or she come away with the sense that God is Holy and to be reverenced?

Or did we cause him to inadvertently blaspheme God because of our misrepresentation of God's holiness?

Our use, or lack of use, of contemporary Christian music is not merely an issue we can decide for ourselves, because the music we choose does have an impact on both our witness and our sanctification.

Nowhere in Scripture are we allowed to decide for ourselves if certain sins are acceptable or not. We may excuse them and ignore our conscience, but in God's eyes they are still sins that need to be dealt with.

Just two verses before this one, Paul has succinctly stated that "every one of us shall give account of himself to God" (verse 12).

When the accounting is accounted for, will our acceptance of CCM, with its clearly identifiable techniques that appeal to our fleshly, carnal self, be acceptable to our Holy God, even if *we* labeled such music "clean"?

1 Thessalonians 5:22 gives us God's viewpoint: "Abstain from all appearance of evil."

34. ". . . *do not let your good be spoken of as evil*" (Rom. 14:16 NKJV).

The use of identifiable, sensual music techniques in Christian music is not a "good" practice.

This is a continuation of the passage mentioned above (Romans 14:14–23). Those who use this argument are claiming that CCM is "good" and that those who say otherwise are calling CCM "evil."

By now, I hope you honestly understand that the use of identifiable, sensual music techniques that appeal to our carnal self is not a good practice. While I understand the thinking and belief that CCM is an acceptable evangelistic tool, it falls far short of having the ability to be called good, simply because of it's carnal appeal to our flesh. Even if the words are good, the vehicle is *not*.

We may think something is good, but when that something is held up to the entire counsel of Scripture, we can see the truth, whether we're right or wrong. And the truth about CCM is that the lyrics are sometimes good, but the musical techniques are never good. And just like partial obedience is still disobedience in God's eyes, CCM with it's worldly, sensual music techniques corrupts the entire package, because as a whole it is not 100 percent righteous.

As we look to the very next two verses in this passage (v. 17–18), we clearly see the real issue: Righteous living, with its resulting peace and joy, is more important to God than those side issues that do not contribute to our personal sanctification, and this has been previously discussed (see numbers 32 and 33 above).

Is CCM evil, or is CCM righteous? I'll let you decide: Do you think God considers it evil to compose and/or sing music that contains techniques that can, and do, cause people to move their bodies sensuously, whether or not that's our motivation? Do you think God considers it righteous to use vocal inflections while singing that would be clearly labeled a come-on in different circumstances?

God warns us in Isaiah 5:20: "Woe to those who call evil good . . ." (NKJV).

35. This is legalism; we now live under grace, because we have liberty in Jesus Christ ("all things are lawful . . .").

We never have liberty to sin, and a desire for personal holiness and sanctification is not legalism. Furthermore, liberty does not mean "license."

I covered this in my first book, but I'd like to briefly provide some additional thoughts.

It would be legalistic if I were to say that we should only sing odd numbered hymns on odd numbered Sundays. Or that we can't use musical instruments in our worship services. Or that anything written after the nineteenth century is sinful. Religious rules and regulations don't change people's sinful hearts. But a heart changed by God's saving grace will result in a desire for personal holiness, and the pursuit of holiness is not legalism. In fact, Jesus expects us to live beyond the Ten Commandments.

For example, while the Ten Commandments tells us, "Thou shalt not commit adultery,"[33] Jesus said, ". . . whoever *looks* at a woman to lust for her has already committed adultery with her in his heart" (Matt. 5:28 NKJV, emphasis mine).

In no way does our freedom in Christ give us the liberty to sin or to live our lives as we see fit, to please ourselves. To the contrary, if we are truly saved, we will increasingly desire personal holiness in every area as we live for the Lord Jesus. We will gladly limit our actions in order to live righteously for Him. And because we are indwelled by the Holy Spirit, we now have the ability and desire to uphold the law.

Romans 3:31 tells us, "Do we then make void the law through faith? God forbid: yea, we establish the law."

Just because Jesus set us free from the Jewish rules and regulations doesn't mean God changed somewhere between the Old and New Testaments: He still requires holiness from His children.[J] Once again, we must understand that the liberty we have as Christians only truly concerns those things in our lives that have no impact on our personal sanctification, that will not be harmful to our testimony, nor cause another person to sin.

So as we apply all of this to contemporary Christian music, can we honestly declare that we have liberty to create or listen to music that pleases our flesh? Do we have liberty to make use of sultry vocal techniques in the name of the Lord Jesus Christ?

The Bible has a warning for those who teach such liberty of the flesh: "While they promise them liberty, they themselves are the servants of corruption: for whom a man is overcome, of the same is he brought in bondage" (2 Pet. 2:19).[K]

Could it be that many are under the bondage of CCM yet don't realize it? Therefore, the terms "legalistic" and "legalism" are quickly applied to the subject of Christian music when the validity of CCM is questioned.

But if we label the desire for righteousness in music as legalism, then we must be prepared to label every form of righteous living as legalistic: abstaining from swearing, alcoholic beverages, and pornography, etc. We can use the legalistic excuse for anything in which we want to continue to participate.

In the entertainment realm, most Christians don't consider it legalistic to eliminate profanity, violence, nudity, and provocative situations from movies. But it would be legalistic to say that all movies are sinful. The same principle applies to music.

We've worried far too much about the issue of legalism, and not enough about our own personal sanctification. It's time that we let God deal with those who are truly legalistic—those who follow religious rules without conviction that comes from a changed heart. But as for ourselves, as born-again believers, we need to get our own hearts serious about pursuing godliness in every area of our lives, and abandon the false notion that taking steps toward personal sanctification is legalistic. It's never legalistic to avoid sin, and it's certainly not legalistic to eliminate sensual (sinful) music techniques in Christian music.

It's true that religious rules don't save us; neither do they aid in our sanctification. Yet Paul gave us a caution about our liberty from the Law that we need to heed: ". . . do not use liberty as an opportunity for the flesh" (Galatians 5:13 NKJV).

In other words, anything that we do in life should not provide us with an opportunity to satisfy our carnal, fleshly self, and that includes actively listening to any music (even

CCM) that appeals to our flesh through carnal, sensual techniques.

36. If CCM offends you, maybe you shouldn't listen to it, but don't put your convictions on everyone else. Let God do the convicting.

Because we are attempting to validate each other's choice of music by continuing to participate in CCM, it has become a *corporate* sin, not only an individual sin; therefore, it *must* be addressed.

This is an important issue: the Holy Spirit's job in convicting us of our sin. One of the reasons that I, and others who stand with me on the issue of CCM, speak out about contemporary Christian music is because we have been given a burden from the Lord. Sometimes, when there is rampant disobedience among God's people, He raises up messengers to warn and instruct them. The Old Testament prophets are a prime example.

By continuing to listen to, write, and/or perform contemporary Christian music, Christians are justifying each other's choice of this type of music. Isn't it easier to excuse our behavior or choice when others are doing it? We all grew up saying that, didn't we? As adults, we're not immune to this excuse.

But this is not just individual sin we are talking about. *This is corporate sin* among God's people at concerts, award ceremonies, and in our churches. This is why the issue of CCM must be addressed.

The CCM industry has become a monster of behemoth proportions. We have dulled our spiritual ears to the calling of the Holy Spirit in the area of music because we like our music—perhaps we even "love" our music.

Which do you love more, your music or God? Would you give up CCM for Him? If not, why not?

37. Our bodies are not sinful.

As a stand-alone physical entity, no. But we can do sinful things with our bodies if we allow our carnal self to submit to temptation.

It is not sinful to fulfill our God-given physical needs in ways that He has deemed righteous; however, each and every desire and physical need must be placed under self-control, which results in righteous behavior within scriptural guidelines and principles.

But we do have a carnal self (also called our flesh in Scripture) that is a separate entity from our physical body. Our flesh is that part of our personality that is still tempted by the pull of sin because it remembers "the pleasures of sin,"[34] and there is a conflict within ourselves between it and our new, regenerate spirit. Our flesh wants us to do whatever we want, whenever we want, and it doesn't want us to behave righteously or with self-control.

We readily understand this struggle when we apply it to food: Do we, or do we not, have that second piece of our favorite dessert? Just as we "remember" a certain food's taste and texture, we also remember the pleasure, excitement, and emotional lift that certain sins temporarily provide for us, and this "remembrance" has a very real and powerful influence on us.

The apostle Paul described this conflict in one succinct verse: "For the flesh lusts against the Spirit, and the Spirit against the flesh; and these are contrary to one another, so that you do not do the things that you wish."

(Gal. 5:17 NKJV) Simply stated, our flesh works contrary to our new life in Christ.

Musically, CCM (and other carnal music) contributes to the feeding of our carnal self, as demonstrated by the way our bodies want to respond with carnal (sensually suggestive) movements. On the other hand, truly spiritual (non-carnal) music will not feed our carnal self, but will encourage us toward righteous behavior.

I will most certainly agree that our bodies are not sinful in and of themselves. But when suggestive body movements are displayed as a response to carnal music techniques, we *do* sin, in both our Christian music and in our bodies, and we are not exhibiting Christ-like character through either. Neither are we obeying Paul's exhortation to "put to death the deeds of the body."[35]

38. What about "moral" music—good, clean music that's just fun for the kids?

It's still rock music, and it's still not training the kids in godly behavior, even though the lyrics may be upright.

While I admire some Christian artists for their stand on certain issues and their attempt to be an example to youth, moral rock music remains a compromise for Christian youth because it doesn't accurately model a set apart life in the biblical sense, which is denial of the carnal self in order to exercise self-control in the spiritual realm, applicable even to teens. It may be moral through the lyrics, but it isn't absolutely moral because of its appeal to the flesh through the music.

In my first book, I showed how the original rock musicians' intentions were to openly promote rebellion, with a focus on the sensual—the body.[36] It was never just a new intellectual musical style, as was the case with most classical music down through history.

But because we have forgotten the wickedness surrounding secular rock music, we now excuse what we had once rejected—namely, rock music with its many layers and styles. We have simply learned to accept rock music as a part of our culture; so now we "work with it," even as Christians.

Our knowledge and acceptance of evil has increased over time and because of this, wisdom that comes from the Lord and being set apart has decreased. Therefore, instead of training our children in righteousness for the Lord, we are actually training them to compromise with the world, with a little morality thrown in.

Music that is labeled "Christian" should, by definition, point people to Christ, through both lyrics and by musical example of pureness. But if morality is the only goal of any music, that doesn't automatically make it Christian, because even unbelievers can be moral.

39. *The Holy Spirit will lead us into all truth. Music is one of them.*

If all we needed were the Holy Spirit, we would have no need for the entire New Testament after the book of Acts (with, perhaps, the exception of Revelation).

2 Timothy 3:16–17 says, "*All* Scripture is given by inspiration of God, and is profitable for doctrine, for reproof, for correction, *for instruction in righteousness,* that the man of God may be complete, thoroughly equipped for every good work" (NKJV, emphasis mine).

Yes, God knew Christians desperately needed instruction in righteous living, and He clearly gave it to us in the form of our New Testament (along with the counsel of the Old Testament).

The Holy Spirit will lead us, but He will never lead us to do anything contrary to Scripture, nor will He lead us to participate in behavior contrary to the holiness and purity of God's character.

40. *What about the mega-churches? Many of them use CCM.*
There are mega-cults, too. Big doesn't necessarily mean God-blessed.

Humanly speaking, "large" is the way we interpret success in America, even among Christians. We evaluate success by the number of people in our pews. Then, success is ours because of our efforts to fill those pews, to reach our goals.

Now I'm not suggesting that the large churches are doing everything wrong. But many pastors have succumbed to the "call" of CCM in order to get a larger crowd, rationalizing that it is a way to get people to come to church.

Using carnal music in the Church does not help a congregation in their personal sanctification, however. Indeed it may be a way to lure people to the Church, but meanwhile, the real fruit has been that the Church has become exactly like the world, rather than the Church being a training ground for believers to become like Jesus—*separate* from the world.

And just because a church appears to be growing, this doesn't necessarily mean we're truly winning people to Christ. Take the contemporary Christian music away and see who is really there to follow Jesus.

41. *But I feel such a freedom to worship with CCM.*

Rock music has been designed to break down our inhibitions. Conversely, God's Word repeatedly tells us to have self-control.[37]

Every true believer already has the ability to have freedom to worship God from his or her heart. The truth is that the rock music, combined with the Christian lyrics, creates an atmosphere where we think we are worshipping better, when in reality we are worshipping less, because of CCM's appeal to our emotional/physical being.

If those same lyrics were sung without the contemporary music, would the level of worship experience be perceived as the same? Probably not, except in a very few individuals. Most people in CCM services are relying on the external addition of the music to help them achieve worship.

Admittedly, musical instrumentation does add beauty to our worship; but if we remove it, there should be no change in our individual worship experience.

42. *What's wrong with drums?*

Nothing, if they're used in their proper place and according to God's principles outlined in the Bible.

Automatically, this excludes any type of rock music, because the use of drums (or bass guitar) in rock music is the primary tool by which carnality is displayed in the music, and ultimately, through the listener's body movements as a response to those drums.

Drums in their proper place, however, add a dimension that can musically exhibit the power, awe, and majesty of God, such as with the use of timpani in an orchestral setting.

And what about the military marches? The drums are crisp and complementary to the music, adding just the right amount of cadence and percussion to command attentiveness and respect from the audience. (Who among us hasn't cheered at a Fourth of July celebration when "Stars and Stripes" was played?)

No, drums in and of themselves are not inherently evil. But their improper use can be sinful.[L]

43. *What about the concern regarding demons and drums?*
While many Christians laugh about this, there is cause to be concerned.

The 1996 November issue of *Travel Holiday* magazine has an interesting article titled, "Voodoo Heart."[38] According to this article, in Guadeloupe, there's a type of music called *gwoka*. The rhythm of the *gwoka* drums is very similar to the drumming associated with Caribbean Revivalist religious ceremonies, which combine voodoo beliefs with elements of Christianity, and as people dance to these rhythms, *demon possession is a common occurrence.*

This type of activity is eerily corroborated in another article, "Hear That Long Snake Moan," from the Spring, 1987, issue of *Whole Earth Review* magazine.[39] In fact, this shocking article explains that the drum is considered holy in Haitian voodoo, and that drummers are well aware that by playing certain rhythms they are many times able to invoke demon possession. Further, this article states that each demon prefers a different rhythm and the drummers know all of them.

The influence of the voodoo religion and its drum rhythms in rock music is well known among secular rock musicians, and they openly recognize the relationship between specific rhythms and demonic activity; they *purposely* study these rhythms.[40, M] Unfortunately, many of God's children have been deceived and refuse to consider that some of these same voodoo rhythms are being used in some contemporary Christian music.

While I am primarily concerned about CCM's appeal to our flesh, I also believe that the concern about the relationship between demons and certain drum rhythms is a real and valid concern, and this phenomenon has actually been witnessed in some American revival services.

God's Word says, "Beloved, believe not every spirit, . . ."[42] and it behooves us to be extremely careful about what goes on in our worship services, for everything is not always as it appears to be.

44. *God can use imperfect vessels for His glory.*

Yes, but because we can clearly identify and manipulate certain musical techniques, His imperfect vessels (true believers) have the *responsibility* to use methods other than those that appeal to the carnal vulnerability of men.

In reality, not one thing or person on earth is exactly perfect, except for the Lord Jesus Christ. The term "imperfect vessel" could mean anything or anyone.

King David was an imperfect vessel, yet God says he was "a man after His own heart."[43] David may have made some sinful mistakes, but when confronted with them, he was convicted and demonstrated true repentance. "Imperfect" does not mean sinful by choice, time after time after time. We may make mistakes, we may stumble, we may sin, but habitual, willful sinning should be foreign to the true Christian.

The term "imperfect vessels" should not be applied to methods that we are able to control: in this instance, Christian music. Our methods may not be exactly perfect, but they can and should be brought under the authority of Scripture to the best of our ability.

Yes, God can use anything as we've previously seen, but He expects us to obey His Word to the best of our imperfect ability in those things over which we *do* have control.

And we do have a choice of whether or not to use carnal, sensual music techniques in our Christian music.

45. Why stir up such controversy? Can't we be tolerant of each other's views? (i.e., since the music issue is not essential to salvation, we should compromise and work together.)

Controversy is necessary for reformation and sin can never be a point of compromise.

A look back through the history of the Church shows this to be true.

The apostle Paul wrote to the Romans in order to clarify the controversy regarding the salvation of both the Jews and the Gentiles. Many of his other epistles also contain portions that addressed controversy about various religious customs and beliefs.

As mentioned previously, Paul's entire message was the subject of much controversy, which resulted in his being stoned, among other things, and even Jesus caused division among people, especially the religious leaders.

More recently, Martin Luther and other Protestant reformers were in the middle of great controversy when they confronted the Roman Catholic Church about some of its practices; finally, they had no choice but to separate themselves.

I will agree that controversy for its own sake is not conducive to righteous living. Controversy where error is practiced and taught, however, is necessary: It challenges people to look at issues that are important to the Church-at-large. Truth will cause division where error exists.

Unfortunately, because CCM has such an appeal to us—such a "hold" on us—this controversy has largely gone unheeded, except by those who are willing "to hear." Those who don't want to hear call for compromise or tolerance.

James 3:17 tells us, "But the wisdom that is from above is *first* pure, then peaceable . . ." (emphasis mine). According to this verse, pureness in our lives and in our congregational worship is to be achieved first, even to the extent of breaking peace, should it be necessary, if others won't hold to standards of purity and righteousness.

But we want to switch the order of this verse; we want peace among our congregations before purity when it comes to CCM. To put it bluntly, the unspoken opinion is, "Put up, or shut up."

In reality, pureness in our lives *will* bring peace; but peace for its own sake will not produce purity.

Therefore, compromise is never a valid choice in the life of a believer in Christ Jesus if sin is involved, and the use of identifiable rock techniques in Christian music—techniques that have been admittedly designed to appeal to our carnal self—is a compromise to sin, not merely a compromise to accept different types of music "in the name of Jesus." It is not a pure form of music.

Ephesians 5:11 puts it this way, ". . . have no fellowship with the unfruitful works of darkness, but rather reprove them." Can we honestly stand before God and say that sensual music techniques are a "fruitful" work?

I agree that this issue is not an essential doctrine for salvation; however, it can affect the issue of salvation, because the likely possibility of "easy believism" offered in the emotional concert environment may result in professions of faith without true *possession* of Christ. Sadly, many people may believe they are saved, but in fact they are not.

And, finally, this issue is definitely an issue of sanctification. Because by promoting or allowing the use of CCM, we're not encouraging sanctification in other people's lives and we're not representing a set apart lifestyle of true Christianity. True love, Paul tells us, is to ". . . Abhor what is evil. Cling to what is good" (Rom. 12:9 NKJV).

Therefore, if any activity is wrong for believers, how can we in good conscience promote its use, even in the name of compromise or evangelism?

46. *There are different worship styles that are acceptable to different types of people.*

Perhaps, but the only worship style that is acceptable to God is one which follows scriptural principles for righteousness and orderliness in *every* area.

Although the New Testament Church no longer follows the Levitical laws, it behooves us to read through Exodus and Leviticus to get a sense of God's interest in the minute details of worship and separated living He required of His people.

As this applies to us, God is no less interested, because He is the One we are worshipping; He should be the One we please, not ourselves. This does not necessarily limit all music to "plainsong,"[N] because, within biblical parameters, we do have a vast array of musical styles which are acceptable for our worship services.

For example, some denominations may prefer a more classical setting, such as music from J.S. Bach or Handel. Others may prefer the down-home flavor of traditional gospel songs. Both are acceptable, because both follow biblical principles outlined in Ephesians 5:19, Colossians 3:16, and other passages regarding holy living.

On the other hand, anyone would have difficulty proving that the Bible says we have the freedom to use identifiable sensual techniques in our worship music as an acceptable worship style.

47. Why can't we just follow the "others may, but I may not" concept? (The flip side of which is, "I may, though others may choose differently," i.e., the Law of Conscience.)

The "others may" statement, and its counterpart, "I may, . . ." can only be applied to areas that are not inherently sinful to begin with, such as bowling or a trip to the amusement park.

The "others-may" concept is applicable only to those activities that, by themselves, are not sinful, harm our testimony, or impede our spiritual growth. For example, bowling is a sport that is not sinful in any way. Because of the atmosphere at most bowling alleys, however, some Christians may choose to refrain from this sport. This is the correct application of the "others-may-I-may-not" philosophy. Most of the time, though, we use the reverse of this maxim to continue to participate in questionable activities, and, unfortunately, most of us are guilty of judging the "other" side—whichever side is the opposite of ours.

We must remember that all of us are at different stages in our Christian growth, but *just because others are participating in questionable or wrong behavior doesn't mean that in God's eyes they may.* The Bible lays out the same standards of holiness for everyone; it's just that some people have been convicted about certain activities and have forsaken them, while others either may have not yet been convicted, or have simply not surrendered to God's promptings.

God has never given any of His children the freedom to sin. Christian music, by definition, should in every aspect model the epitome of the sanctified Christian life, according to God's Word.

Yet it has been proven that CCM does contain sinful musical techniques and these techniques do not aid in our personal sanctification toward holiness—to the contrary. Therefore, we cannot rightly apply the "others-may-but-I-may-not" (or vice versa) adage.

48. Like other periods in history, CCM is just a new music of our times—nothing more—and will eventually be totally accepted into the Church.

Never before in the history of Western civilization has there been such a blatant focus on the seductive/sensual, and, certainly, secular music (rock, jazz, etc.) reflects this. Unfortunately, by imitating rock music, contemporary Christian music also focuses on these areas.

We've become so desensitized that we no longer recognize this as sin, and sensuality even appears throughout children's media—toys, video games, music, cartoons, advertisements, and magazines. *Anything experienced over and over becomes acceptable after a time.*

But it's not acceptable to God, even though it may be acceptable to us. In reality, by accepting CCM as just another style of church music, Christians are only revealing how far away we've moved from God's Word and the pursuit of holiness in our lives.

49. We just need to keep an open mind. We shouldn't be afraid of new musical styles and expressions.

Not everything that is new is biblically sound.

While it is a valid argument that we shouldn't be so set in our ways that we miss some true blessings, by the way of innovative ideas in our lives (or music), we need to also be aware that all things must pass under the scrutiny of biblical principles before they can be accepted.

The phrase "open mind" should be a red flag to any believer, because it is a term that secular society throws around to excuse sinful behavior or non-biblical practices.

The Bible tells us that Christians "have the mind of Christ."[45] What would our Lord Jesus Christ's mind be concerning CCM? Would He applaud the carnal appeal of the musical techniques even though the lyrics were "good"? Would He dance in the carnal fashion that such music provokes? Would He sing in the suggestive manner CCM vocalists use?

Finally, I've been asked, *"How do you know you're right?"* My answer is to return a question: "When has God's Word ever commanded or encouraged us to use sensual methods, which appeal to our carnal, fleshly self, for worship, evangelism, ministry, personal edification, or sanctification?" Answer: Never.

This has been a necessarily long chapter, and unbelievably, there are still a few "excuses" that will be covered in other chapters. While there will probably be those Christians who will continue to disagree about CCM for some reason or the other, in each statement we can easily see that what we believe is our "truth." Our personal truth frames our perspective of life, including our philosophy of acceptable Christian music.

Additionally, we tend to adhere to our own belief system, no matter what, because our personal pride and preferences are at stake. Because of this, we're guilty of the same practice evolutionists follow; they throw out evidence that doesn't support their beliefs, so that they can continue to make their own "truth." But as Christians, are we to believe what *we* think; are we to "lean to our own understanding,"[46] or believe what the *Bible* says?

What is your truth? Does what you believe about music (not just the lyrics) line up with the *whole* counsel of the Bible regarding purity and righteousness? Can you prove scripturally that the identifiable, carnal music techniques used in CCM are "acceptable to God"?[47] Or will you throw out everything the Bible says about righteous living as it applies to music?

In answering some of these statements, I challenged that we take away CCM to see what people's true response to the Lord Jesus would be.

What would *your* personal response be? Defensiveness? Anger? Rebellion? Or sweet submission to God? The answer will show the true heart of the reader, for Jesus tells us in His Word, "If you love Me, keep My commandments" (John 14:15 NKJV), and again He says in John 14:23, ". . . If anyone loves Me, he will keep My word . . ." (NKJV).[48]

Will you keep God's Word regarding holiness and purity in all of your music? Would you be willing to remove CCM or any other wrong music from your life?

And if they took the music away, would you *still* follow Jesus?

Chapter Four Notes

A. In the video seminar, *The Language of Music*, Dr. Frank Garlock relates an account of an organization which claimed 1000 people were saved at a particular Christian rock festival. A few months later, however, this same organization sent out representatives to visit with those who said they had made professions of faith. *They did not find one single person whom they believed had been truly converted to Christ.*[1]

B. True salvation will result in a changed life. See chapter five.

C. *Moshpits* are areas in which a crowd of young people gather to "dance" by crashing into each other. Moshing, also called body slamming or slamdancing, can be very aggressive and violent—resulting in concussions, bloody noses, and other serious injuries. This type of activity is simply the sensual gone chaotic/frenzied, and occurs at some CCM concerts—even in churches.

D. See chapter nine, as well as Appendix One, for application of this.

E. Ideas for parents to help their teens are in chapter nine.

F. See chapter three and Appendix Three for these specific techniques.

G. See chapter three and Appendix Three.

H. See Appendix One for further styles to explore as well as suggestions for listening.

I. In the KJV, Philippians 4:5 uses the word *moderation*, however the Greek actually means gentle or patient behavior, not, as supposed, allowing for moderate tolerance or practice of questionable, or borderline, activities; neither could it be construed to mean that we are able to participate in just anything, so long as we do so without excess, or to the extreme.

J. While we are declared righteous and justified, solely through the atoning blood of Christ Jesus, when we place our faith in Him, we should also be applying active holiness in our lives, removing those things from our lives that God shows us, so that we may further our personal sanctification—pornography, swearing, immodest clothing, wrong behavior, etc.

K. Read verse 18 along with verse 19.

L. NOTE: Some would debate that because no mention is made in the New Testament of any musical instrument being used in worship, we shouldn't use them in today's Church. I disagree. If the use or non-use of instruments in worship had been an issue that affected our sanctification, God would have given specific directions as He did with the kind of music we are to sing (spiritual songs). And 2 Timothy 3:16 states, "All Scripture . . . is profitable. . . ."

M. Jeff Godwin, of "The Rock Ministries," has compiled and documented a long list of secular artists who have traveled to foreign countries in order to study and learn voodoo drum rhythms.[41]

N. *Plainsong* is a simple melody sung without accompaniment. Although early New Testament church music began as plainsong, ancient musical notations called *cantillation signs*, deciphered from the Hebrew Scriptures, indicate surprisingly complex music which accompanied the Hebrew text.[44]

CHAPTER FIVE

"COOL" IS NOT A FRUIT OF THE SPIRIT

". . . what is highly esteemed among men
is an abomination in the sight of God."
Luke 16:15 NKJV

A bout fifteen years ago I was on the other side of this issue. I thought CCM was the newest revelation from God! It was a cool sound that fit right in with my musical tastes. I could really worship God (or so I thought) but like many people today, I simply didn't understand what God's perspective was, or what the Bible said. I was only aware of my own feelings, emotions, and thoughts; I was a relatively new Christian.

I grew up going to church off and on. At one point, when I was around twelve years old, I made a profession of faith but didn't really understand what that meant. In the years to follow, I would occasionally rededicate my life, but again, other than trying to do better each time in my own strength, nothing really changed in my life.

When I read my Bible, I could never get past the four Gospels. Now I realize that until true salvation occurred, I couldn't understand anything else.

I moved away from home and went to college. I tried to find a church, but still, I didn't attend regularly, and really nothing clicked, other than I'd better be "good." I loved disco music, and I loved to dance. (I had not only had several years of ballet and tap dance training, I had also taken classes in jazz dance, so I know what I speak about when I talk about body movement to music.)

During my first year of college, I declared my major as piano performance. Prior to college, I had already had eleven years of piano lessons and had accompanied flute and vocal soloists and two school choirs. Additionally, I had moderate experience in school bands and competitions playing percussion instruments: bells, chimes, marimba, cymbals, timpani, and I had even taken a few lessons in snare drums!

As my college career moved forward, I decided to switch majors to Speech and Dramatic Art with an emphasis in radio-TV-film production. My main motivation was that I wanted to put music to film sequences. (I had been inspired by the first *Rocky* movie.) I loved my new major because I could be so creative, yet I continued taking music courses, piano and jazz band, as well as accompanying extracurricular choirs.

During all of this time, I thought I was saved and even knew how to share with others that they needed a Savior. However, I truly did not have a love for the things of the Lord. I had, instead, a love for the things of the world.

It wasn't until the fall of 1982, after college and marriage, that I came to know the Lord Jesus Christ in a real and personal way. He did such a work in my heart that now I know without a doubt I was not saved before, even though I had been religious and fairly good (not perfect, just good in the world's way of thinking). Looking back, though, I consider my life then as very sinful. My pastor likes to say that when we truly become saved, we "love what we used to hate, and hate what we used to love." This is so very true.

And so, God began working in my heart and life. I reluctantly switched from secular rock to CCM. At that time, the CCM I listened to was nothing like the range of CCM available now. It was just beginning to catch up to secular rock, with a little "cutting edge" music thrown in here and there.

Some of you reading this will say, "See! There's a place for CCM. You've just proved that it can help as a transition from secular life to Christian life." I disagree, and so will my husband, who, *even as an unbeliever, thought that CCM was totally wrong*. Did you get that? Someone on the outside, looking in, so to speak, thought that CCM was wrong for Christians! (He's a believer now.) I'll share why I disagree in a moment.

I had begun to understand that secular rock music was wrong for Christians, but didn't equate my CCM with secular rock. As I stated at the beginning of this chapter, I thought CCM was the best thing to happen to Christian music. If someone had shared with me what I know now, there is no way I would have agreed! Just like most people, I wouldn't have been able to hear anything sensual in the music, either. Yet God continued to work.

Slowly the lights began to go on in my spirit and mind. I began to see that some CCM was probably not right, and I was very careful about which CCM I did choose.

I got busy with babies, and had less and less time to pop music into the tape player, other than cute music for the kids. Although, as I ran errands around town, I'd either listen to the classical music station, or the soundtrack to the motion picture, *Glory,* (on which the Harlem Boys' Choir sing and that has some very good music). I realize now that God was providing me with a "music fast."[A] Finally, I became uncomfortable when I listened to my conservative CCM. It was time to give it up.

It wasn't until God burdened me to write *Oh, Be Careful Little Ears,* that I could really articulate all that I felt. During the writing of that book, I cried out to God over and over to show me the truth about music. It was an emotional roller coaster because I was forced to look at every side of this issue, but it was also such a blessing to have it all nailed down and written so that others could be helped, too. Not only did it strengthen my convictions about music, it strengthened my personal faith.

I write all of this so that you might understand that the area of musical discernment is a process; it rarely comes overnight. Especially so because we've been so saturated with various styles of rock music throughout our culture, as well as within the Christian realm. But discernment will never come if we're not open to the Lord working in our lives in this area; if we're not willing to change our ideas.

Do I still struggle? Yes. If I hear a song from my past, it pulls up all of the old garbage that went with that point in time. I can understand that, and accept it, though. Every true believer in Christ Jesus will struggle until we receive our redeemed bodies that are no longer subject to the pull of this sinful world.[1]

What I cannot accept is the fact that most CCM can pull up those same kinds of feelings because CCM uses those *same* secular rock music techniques, powerful techniques that call to the carnal, fleshly self, no matter what the words. As with secular rock music, I feel the pull of the world when I listen to CCM.

This is an important fact to realize. This is why CCM cannot be pleasing to God, Who wants us to overcome our flesh[2] and be conformed to the image of His Son.[3] God wants His best for us, even if it's not "cool" in the world's way of thinking.

Let's face it, all of us are fearful of not being accepted, of not being like everyone else. Oh, we claim to be different because we're Christians, but we still want to be cool within the parameters of Christendom, and CCM gives us the arena in which to be cool. We can sing like the world, we can dance like the world, we can act like the world, all under the umbrella of Christianity, with CCM as our musical conduit. CCM now makes it cool to attend church because in many of today's churches there is cool music.

The Bible says, "Love not the world, neither the things that are in the world. If any man love the world, the love of the Father is not in him. For all that is in the world, the lust of the flesh, and the lust of the eyes, and the pride of life, is not of the Father, but is of the world" (1 John 2:15–16).

This verse is not simply or only talking about things we can see or touch, those physical things that money can buy and that sometimes we actually need. This verse also implies the worldly *attitudes* in our lives, attitudes such as the underlying sensuality prevalent in much contemporary

Christian music, unbiblically cool or rebellious attitudes conveyed through worldly Christian music videos and concerts, and other attitudes that come right out of our ungodly world system.

This brings me to the second reason I have for sharing my testimony: I want people to realize that just because we might know some things about Christianity, listen to Christian music, go to church, and know how to share Christ with others, even appear religious, these things do not ensure we are true believers. I, myself, thought that I was truly saved, only to find out as a young adult that I wasn't. I was "of the world," according to the above verse. I wanted to be cool and yet religious at the same time.

How does one know for a certainty that he or she belongs to the Lord? There are evidences in our lives: a love for the things of the Lord, a desire to live a holy life, a love for others and a concern for their salvation, conviction of specific sin in our lives (not just general moral convictions—specific sin) and an increasing abhorrence of sin, true repentance, a love for God's Word, an overwhelming desire to uphold and defend God's reputation, and a desire to please Him in all that we do.

Pastor John MacArthur has a booklet titled *Examine Yourself*, and I recommend obtaining a copy for yourself or a loved one, as it discusses this important topic of true salvation.[B]

I mentioned earlier in this chapter that I disagree that CCM can be used as a transition from secular life to the Christian life. While an argument for transitional use may be made, there are several reasons why it should not be so used.

First, CCM, as I have defined it (Christian music which makes use of sensual music techniques and rhythms), is unbiblical for the simple reason that it appeals to the flesh, whereas God desires that we "put to death the deeds of the body."[4] Are we truly living according to the Spirit and putting our flesh "to death" if we are listening to or writing music (not the lyrics) that appeals to that flesh?

Second, it hinders and sometimes blocks the new believer's progress into holiness, which God desires for each of us,[5] and deadens his or her discernment in the area of music—the result of which most Christians stay in the CCM realm because they've become accustomed to the flesh-appealing nature of the music. Consequently, there is no application made in the musical domain regarding the struggle between our new life in Christ and our carnal self—a struggle that we should readily experience elsewhere in life. We simply accept CCM without question, giving in to our carnal self just as we did in response to secular rock music before Christ came into our life. Carnal music produces carnal Christians, promoting and encouraging carnality in many new and "older" Christians because it can prevent them from growing beyond "babes in Christ."[6]

Third, it sends a mixed message that is confusing to both unbelievers and believers alike—that music is an area of Christian living where the rules are different. "Anything goes" musically as long as the words are morally upright.

Finally, as with any other wrong habit in our lives, which we know is not pleasing to God, "cold turkey" is the best approach to removing that habit. For with sins such as alcoholism or pornography, we never, ever counsel that a person drink less and less, until finally, a person is "dry"; neither do we tell those involved in pornography to just look at less and less pornography, until finally they're able to give it up entirely. To counsel in this manner for both of these examples would be contrary to Scripture's teaching to "make no provision for the flesh."[7]

Similarly, we cannot reasonably use CCM as a bridge to a pure style of Christian music and the committed Christian life because contemporary Christian music retains remnants from an old lifestyle—remnants that speak of sensuality and worldliness. And because of these influences, a person is subtly discouraged from pressing on in their new life in Christ, a life that should at the outset begin to strive toward holiness and separateness, even in our music. And from the outset, a person should begin to discern, not only in music, but in other areas of life.

I stated at the beginning of this chapter that as a new believer I thought CCM was a new revelation from God. Now I know the opposite is true: The techniques used in most CCM are subtle tools of Satan—tools that feed our pride, our flesh, and our emotions. They are tools that satisfy the unspoken desire (and sometimes unrecognized desire) that we wish to be cool at all costs.

But "cool" is not a fruit of the Spirit.[8]

Chapter Five Notes

A. See chapter nine.

B. "Grace to You" Ministries. See Appendix One, "Books/Booklets," for further information.

THE COME-CASUAL CHURCH

"The fear of the Lord is the beginning of wisdom:
and the knowledge of the Holy is understanding."
Proverbs 9:10

An offshoot of the contemporary Christian music movement has been the proliferation of casual worship services across this land in the last few years of the twentieth
century and into the twenty-first century.

The thinking goes like this: "There's a whole generation of unchurched people. They'd feel more comfortable
coming to church if church wasn't so 'stuffy.' We really need
to reach these people, so let's have a casual service: 'Come
as you are.' After all, God looks at the heart."

The pastor wears no tie, and unbuttons the top button
of his shirt (if he even *wears* a dress shirt). People show up
in sweats, shorts, jeans, and everyday, run-of-the-mill clothing. Is God honored?

While I would agree that the Bible nowhere states that "Thou shalt wear only thy best clothing to worship service," God was very specific about how the Old Testament priests were to prepare themselves before they came to serve Him. They were to wash, be anointed, and wear specific clothing.[1] This was a major ritual.

Of course, we now understand that Jesus did away with the ceremonial washings and purifications and now is concerned with our heart condition. But there are a few questions and concerns that arise regarding how we present ourselves for worship.

It's a well known and researched fact that people perform best in the workplace, in school, and in social situations when they are dressed nicely. We seem to live up to our clothing, or live down, as the case may be. For example, do you feel at your best when you're in your Saturday grubbies? Would you want to address our national Senate floor dressed this way? Would you be taken seriously, even if your heart was right?

Imagine you are selected to meet the President of the United States. And let's imagine he or she is of your own political preference and could do no wrong in your eyes. Would you show up in everyday clothing? Unless you positively could not help it, no. And even if you truly had nothing decent to wear, you'd worry about your appearance.

My husband is an attorney. In no possible way would he let his client show up for a trial dressed shabbily, even if he had to buy clothing for that client.

It's interesting to learn that in every seminar my husband has attended regarding trial practice, the point has been stressed that the client's appearance is extremely important, having an effect on both judges and juries. Judges and juries know that the way a person is dressed speaks strongly of that person's character and attitude. The type of clothing a person wears indicates whether or not the person on trial respects them and takes the trial seriously.

And as judges require and deserve the respect of their office, so does the President of the United States, as do each of our elected officials.[A] This is a simple fact of life.

But somehow we've decided that God is different. In our zeal to evangelize the millions, we've lost this idea of respect for God and His position. We can go to church on Sundays (or Saturday evenings) in everyday clothes. But we wouldn't dream of wearing those same clothes to meet the President of the United States.

Why is God different? Doesn't God deserve *more* respect than the President?

Biblically, when Joseph was brought out of prison to interpret the Pharaoh's dream, he shaved, and *changed clothes* before he went to Pharaoh.[3] This was an act of respect.

Likewise, when Queen Esther was preparing to appeal to King Ahasuerus regarding her people, she dressed in her "royal apparel."[4] This was also done out of respect for the king and his position.

Yes, we all are familiar with 1 Samuel 16:7, ". . . for man looks at the outward appearance, but the LORD looks at the heart"(NKJV). This was spoken by God to Samuel when Samuel was sent to anoint David as Israel's king and is in reference only to physical attributes, not to clothing.[B]

Years later, we see in 2 Samuel 12:20, after learning that his first child with Bathsheba had died, David ". . . arose from the earth, and washed, and anointed himself, and *changed his apparel*, and came into the house of the LORD, and worshipped . . ." (emphasis mine). Doesn't this demonstrate that the shepherd boy's heart, now as king, had a desire to respect and honor God? Shouldn't our outward appearance also reflect our heart's desire to honor God?

Once again, we have taken another Scripture out of its original and intended use in order to justify and excuse our actions. Week after week we claim that it's our heart condition that matters to God. That's all. If our heart is right, if we are there to worship Him "in spirit and in truth,"[5] nothing else matters to God. Or so we think.

Can't we even make an effort to dress nicely for worship services before a Holy God Who sent His precious Son Jesus Christ to pay the price of death for our sins? What kind of effort did His death require? What kind of agony did both the Father and the Son experience at the Cross so that we could be reconciled to God? How can we treat this event so lightly that we now decide we'll wear ragged jeans or shorts to our worship services?

Indeed, I think it *does* matter to God; may He have mercy upon our sorry ways.

Furthermore, worship is for the believers. How can nonbelievers worship God Whom they don't know personally? We, as believers, need to be setting an example for unbelievers; an example that by our clothing, as well as our behavior, we show respect and honor to a Holy God. A God who is righteous, pure, just, loving, and perfect in every way. A good God Who deserves our best. A God Who loved us so much that He made a way for us to be forgiven of our sins. We shouldn't let our comfort, or the comfort of others, be more important than reflecting God's glory in our appearance. We shouldn't let our comfort be more important than honoring God with our best.

Of course, if someone visits our church wearing torn or ragged clothing we should understand that God is "no respecter of persons," and neither should we be.[6] But as believers in Christ, we can demonstrate our own personal respect for God through our clothing, while at the same time show mercy toward others.

Yes, we do reflect God's glory in our appearance if we're true believers. Is God a shabby God? I think not. Is He a lazy God? Decidedly not. And I doubt that He's a casual God, either. Would you want Him to have a casual attitude toward your personal circumstances when those circumstances were really bad?

Yet it appears that our degree of preparation for worship (our effort) demonstrates the degree of respect we have for God. Indeed, our dress does communicate what is in our heart; it is the outward sign of our inward heart condition.

I'm not saying we should spend hours and hours in front of the mirror, nor am I suggesting one go into debt to buy fancy clothes. And, of course, a small farming community will dress differently than an upscale, big-city suburb. But in every case there should be an effort made to honor the Lord through the outward appearance of clothing.

God is interested in the best that each of us individually have to offer Him, not how we compare to others. *He* knows what our best is. *He* knows if we come to church with a casual attitude or an attitude of respect.

And if our hearts are truly wanting to honor God, we will want to honor Him with the clothing we wear as we come before Him to worship.

Certainly we may have casual Bible studies and casual fellowships; mission-oriented meetings have their place, too. There's nothing wrong with these. But our weekly corporate worship at our established community churches should be a time that we set apart, that we make an effort, to outwardly demonstrate to God our love and respect for who He is. If we really love Him as we say we do, it seems that we'd want to outwardly show that love by dressing nicely. We do many other things in our daily lives to outwardly demonstrate our love for friends and family. Why not for God?

Our excuse, though, is that God knows our hearts. Yes, He does—better than we do.[7] He knows that our dressing up is too much to ask, that our comfort is more important than His majesty and His worth.

If you are a pastor of a come-casual church, I'm sure you've made the decision to offer this casual approach to worship after much prayer and study. Not one of us is infallible, however, and we can actually sometimes make decisions that are not God's perfect will, even after much prayer and counsel. Every one of us is still subject to the deceitfulness of our flesh and can be swayed by human reasoning, pride, circumstances, research, church politics, and the need for more people because more money is required to pay the bills.

But there is such a thing as false peace.

Sure people come—lots of people. It's easy if we don't have to dress up, it's convenient if we can just drop in, and it's great that the music is exciting and upbeat. But remember, God tells us in His Word that, "The fear [reverence] of the LORD is the *beginning* of wisdom . . ."[8] (emphasis mine). If we're not showing reverence to the Lord by our choice of clothing for corporate worship, where do we begin our quest for wisdom from the Lord? Can we make up for a casual or sloppy appearance by demonstrating reverence and respect elsewhere in our lives? Where else, and how else, could we show reverence? Will God overlook our lack of reverence in the simple area of appropriate clothing for corporate worship if we're more reverent in other areas? Which areas? And how much more reverent?

It seems to me that we would want to show respect and honor to the Lord in every area possible, not just our hearts—that's only the beginning—and our appearance for corporate worship is an easy area through which to outwardly demonstrate the reverence in our hearts.

And pastors, does the clothing you wear for corporate worship set an example of reverence for God to your congregation? Or do you seek to make the congregation "comfortable" by dressing like they do? Which is it to be—the congregation, or God? There are occasions when we must stand for God regardless of who we might offend, and corporate worship is the exact place and time where we should honor Him alone and no one else.

So we must now ask an important question: "If we took away the upbeat music and required a modicum of respectful clothing, would people still attend our services; would they still follow Jesus?"

If we could possibly be bold enough to ask (and apply) these considerations, the true believers would be revealed—those who are coming to truly worship God, in contrast to those who are coming for the excitement of the service as well as for the "extra benefits" the church has to offer, similar to many who followed Jesus, but when the preaching got tough, deserted Him.[9]

Yet how many times has it been said, "Everyone's using CCM; everyone's offering casual worship services"?

Biblically, the majority is usually wrong. Look at every one of the Old Testament prophets. Not one of them was accepted by the majority of God's people. Look at the apostles, most of which, if not all, suffered martyrdom, imprisonment, or exile from the very hands of religious people. And not all people who claim to serve Jesus are true Christians.[10]

Do you know what has really happened—the true reason why we are offering casual worship services? It's because the emphasis in our services has shifted from affirming the holiness of God to dressing to conform to the musical standards and attitudes revealed through the rock music techniques evident in CCM. Just like no one dresses up to go to a secular rock concert, where loose attitudes abound, the Church now also allows people to dress down to the music rather than up to show respect for God's character and Who He is.

By dressing to conform to the lower musical standards, we've once again demonstrated our lack of denial of our flesh, which is naturally lazy. And by offering casual worship services, we are actually conditioning people to give in to their lazy nature; we are encouraging them to feed their flesh, rather than deny it so that they may live victoriously in Him, which is what God desires.

This lack of denial of our carnal, fleshly self is most likely the main cause of our acceptance of both the come-casual church and the sensual music that we have allowed into our churches. Our acceptance of one (flesh-pleasing music) made it easy to accept the other (casual clothing), and there are further ramifications to the Church-at-large, which will be addressed in the following chapters.

Perhaps this chapter's message is "a hard saying; who can hear it?"[11] But God's ways are not our ways, and indeed, Jesus Himself said, "Enter by the narrow gate; for wide is the gate and broad is the way that leads to destruction, and there are many who go in by it. Because narrow is the gate and difficult is the way which leads to life, and there are few who find it" (Matt. 7:13–14 NKJV).

Will *you* "have ears to hear"?

Chapter Six Notes

A. We may not agree with an elected official's behavior or political policy; nevertheless, the Bible says we are to respect their office.[2]

B. NOTE: In the 1 Samuel 16:1–13 passage, David had been tending sheep when he was anointed, he was not formally worshipping the LORD.

CHAPTER SEVEN

THE SECULARIZATION
OF THE CHURCH

*"Tell My people their transgression,
And the house of Jacob their sins."*
Isaiah 58:1 NKJV

In the fall of 1999, I attended a Christian crusade, and while the choir sang the first song, the people in the arena did the "wave." You know, where each section takes turns quickly standing up with their hands in the air. And this continues all around the stadium or arena, whichever the case may be.

Prior to this, people had been chanting back and forth across the arena, similar to activities at a sporting event, trying to "out spirit" the other side. Of course, they used spiritual chants, which included the name of our beloved Lord Jesus.

While most people would probably think of these activities as just good clean fun, I beg to differ. It was like we were all somewhere just having a good time, and then out of the blue, a preacher decided to step up to the microphone and deliver a sermon.

But everyone in that arena *knew* why we were there—to praise and worship God and hear testimonies and a message about our Lord Jesus Christ. Did they act like it? No.

Yet, if we had behaved like this forty years ago, it would have been recognized as seriously wrong for Christians. What is the difference? Only the time in history. Did God change His expectations of our behavior at a Christian meeting, just because we're now in a different period of history? I doubt it.

I call it "the secularization of the Church," and one of its direct causes is that God's people have not been diligent guards in the area of Christian music. This lack of diligence (together with our lack of self-denial), and the resulting thinking that goes along with rock music, has bled over into the rest of our lives.

Recall the story of the frog that was placed in a pan of cool water. Feeling comfortable, he remained, not realizing that the water was slowly heating to the boiling point; not realizing that he would soon be boiled to death, yet he remained compliant because the change was ever so gradual.

Today's Church is exactly like that frog which has been slowly boiled to death because we have allowed the world to slowly infiltrate the Church to an alarming degree, and it all began with our acceptance of the world's music. Just like the frog's water temperature, the change in our churches was very subtle at first, until now we have the extreme: full-blown "Christian" concerts that include slamdancing, among other things.

Little do we realize that music has an influence upon us that goes far beyond the words we are trying to convey. And with the secularization of the Church-at-large, not only have we adopted the rock music of secular society, we have also acquired the thoughts, attitudes, actions, and behaviors that go along with it. We have allowed the world's music to shape our reasoning, and we tend to believe our reasoning *more* than the Word of God.

Carte blanche acceptance of CCM has not only dulled our discernment in the area of music, it has also dulled our spiritual discernment in other areas of life. Furthermore, our promotion of CCM simply makes secular rock acceptable and excusable, and there are no lines of demarcation anymore in the area of music among most Christian people.

It can be seen in the eyes of our youth, as well as in the eyes of all those who listen to CCM on a regular basis. To use the vernacular, its called *attitude*. Sometimes it can be seen as rebellion in the eyes, sometimes it's just a "darkness." Whichever it is, it is exactly the look that unbelievers caught up in secular rock or jazz music have in their eyes, too.

Pay attention to the album covers the next time you visit a Christian bookstore. Look at the eyes of the artists. Ninety percent of them will be as I have described. Some will also have a come-hither look.

Is this right among those who call themselves Christian? Do these album cover photos exhibit sweetness of spirit and love for others? Do you see Christ-likeness in the eyes, or worldly attitudes? Yet we allow, and even promote, this type of music—and the attitudes that go along with it—"in the name of Jesus."

As I was growing up in the '60's and early-to-mid '70's, only a few kids had that "bad girl" or "bad boy" look on their faces. Today, the opposite is true. Everywhere in secular society this is promoted as the norm. Most any catalog or magazine will show the children/youth models with the "look," not to mention the presence of this attitude throughout television and other media.

But what's true in secular society is now also true within the Church-at-large. Just as the secular culture changed with the advent of rock 'n' roll, our Christian culture has changed with our acceptance of CCM—and *neither* culture has changed for the better.

Look around at the youth group at your church. The larger the church, the more this is true; and the more CCM is promoted at church, the eyes of our kids (and even the adults) are clouded, or defensive, at the very least.

I'm not interested in *Raising PG Kids in an X-Rated Society*.[1] I'm interested in training my children in God's ways— in righteousness and purity.[2] But it seems that many Christians are just happy to get their children raised. And when the children act foolishly, how many times have we heard the excuse, "It's just a phase they're going through"?

Nevertheless, the accepted youthful "phase" of CCM has now permeated the Church, the result of which has been a lowering of standards for the Christian. No longer do we seek to pursue righteousness; we seek instead, worldliness.

I recently reviewed a new album by a well-known Christian artist. This album has been highly promoted among Christians. Yet this work had only one mention of God in passing, and the lyrics were all very you-and-me, touchy-feely, with perhaps a very few double-entendre meanings that *might* be construed as referencing God. If someone who didn't know anything about God was listening to this music, however, he or she might well have concluded that this music spoke about someone's girlfriend. In all actuality, this album, as well as much CCM, is really only secular rock music by a Christian artist.

And we wonder why our kids and the Church-at-large are so worldly!

Moreover, we *promote* these worldly attitudes in Christian publications, workshops, and retreats targeted directly at the youth. We say we are countering our secular culture in an effort to help our youth through those difficult years, but the truth is that we are encouraging them to *imitate* the culture around us, only in a Christian manner, with a Christian attitude. In reality, we are attempting to lower God to their level, rather than encouraging them to live up to His standards of holiness and purity; standards which do require a separateness from the sinful attitudes and actions of our culture.

Allowing and advocating these attitudes will work as a detriment to our youth and the Church, because one day, these same youth will be our Church leaders. When I am elderly, I won't want a worldly preacher with an attitude delivering a feel-good sermon from the pulpit week after week. Will you?

Our lack of diligence and self-denial in the area of music, with the resulting tolerance, acceptance, and promotion of contemporary Christian music, have been major catalysts for our secularization. Why? Because we have been, and are, guilty of worshipping the music, rather than worshipping God. So much so that we refuse to give it up and we make up all kinds of excuses—justifications—for its continued use.

As an illustration, let's return to the crusade mentioned earlier. During a CCM artist's performance, a woman seated close to me stood up, and with her hand in the air, palm facing out, sang along with the music. People around her would think she was praising God. Yet I have seen this *exact* posture used by secular artists, singing secular music. Are *they* worshipping God? It's very doubtful. It appears that they are worshipping the music, and I suggest that we, too, are, many times, worshipping the music, rather than worshipping Holy God at CCM concerts, as well as in worship services that use contemporary Christian music.

We have defined how God wants to be worshipped according to our likes, not according to guidelines and principles He has set forth in Scripture.[3] We are trying to conform God to *our* standards rather than submit to His. And we have projected *our* feelings and ideas about music and worship unto Jesus, but not a single one of us knows without a doubt what He thinks, other than what is revealed to us in Scripture. Shouldn't we apply those Scriptures and scriptural principles to our music, using the whole counsel of the Bible, so that we may faithfully comply with God's standards? And *nowhere* in Scripture are we given permission for unconditional use of any questionable or sinful practice in order to reach the lost or to make use of in worship. God doesn't need this kind of help in order to draw people to Himself.

Has it occurred to us to consider what God prefers in worship? After all, we are worshipping Him. Shouldn't we please God Who does so much for us, instead of focusing on our own experience, or on how many people we can get to our church service? We should be rightly focusing on God and giving Him the attention He deserves.

And the answer to this question of pleasing Him in worship is found in Scripture, if we'd only care to look. It's not right to pray about something (e.g., CCM) if it's contrary to Scripture. But because we've used our own faulty reasoning as an attempt to excuse our lack of diligence, to excuse our lack of denial of wrong music in our lives, the Church has become worldly and secularized.

Another place our acceptance of contemporary Christian music has contributed toward the secularization of the Church is in the church sanctuary.

If you are over forty, maybe you remember a time when the church sanctuary was just that—a sanctuary. A quiet place where one could sit and ponder the things of the Lord: where one could pray. A place far removed from the cares of the world, so that, indeed, our souls could find sanctuary and refuge from worldly pursuits.

Children were admonished to not run in church, men removed their hats at the church door, and during the organ prelude, people quietly prepared their hearts for worship.

The sanctuary was a place where God met with us individually and corporately. It was a place where we could experience an almost tangible cleansing from the filth of the world. We expected our church sanctuary to be different from other places.

All that has changed now, especially among many modern-day, evangelical churches. The sanctuary has now become an auditorium—a stage for concerts, dramas, musicals, dance presentations, and performances of all types.

While the coming of Jesus Christ necessarily did away with the ceremonial laws, regulations, and rituals, His coming in no way negated the reverence and respect we should have for God. A reverence which in former days was demonstrated by our attitude about our church's sanctuary.

As New Testament believers, we understand that God no longer chooses to dwell in a building or special place because He now indwells us through the Holy Spirit,[4] yet there is something special about a place "set apart" for God, a place that is different from the world.

A couple of summers ago, my family visited Savannah, Georgia. While there, we decided to go into the Cathedral. It was beautiful on the inside, but more importantly, there was a distinct atmosphere of reverence. People whispered if they chose to speak, and the entire sanctuary commanded the visitors' respect and awe for God. Those who were there to pray weren't hindered by children running up and down the aisles nor by loud conversation. Hospitals also have a similar quietness and reverence in their chapels.

Have you ever been outside, just enjoying the fresh air and listening to the hum of insects and the twitter of birds, away from people, cars, phones, and cares of this world, and felt the peacefulness? Maybe a peaceful place for you is by the ocean, listening to the waves crash against the beach. Or you might enjoy the gentle movement and quiet lapping of the water while on a boat in the middle of a lake. Aren't these wonderful, peaceful experiences?

During the writing of my first book, my family took our summer pilgrimage to Mackinac Island, Michigan. There is a church there called The Little Stone Church, originally built as a mission, and it is simply a one-room sanctuary/church, very nicely and traditionally furnished now.

One day during the week we stepped inside, and, by God's loving providence, the organist was practicing hymns for an upcoming service. We sat down to listen, and the peace and calm that enveloped us in that small chapel was such that we didn't want to leave. To go outside into the "real world" was a letdown to our spirits because we felt safe and secure and in God's presence in that small sanctuary. Our souls felt cleansed from the world and all the temptations and sins it holds. We experienced a very real reverence for God there that day, even though there wasn't a worship service.

Do you experience similar inward peace and reverence for God prior to, or during, your worship service in this twenty-first century? If we are true believers, our souls will increasingly long to be in the presence of God, and absent from the presence of sin. And an earthly church sanctuary can at least partially provide for this desire of our hearts.

Do you get a sense of God's comfort and protection in the sanctuary of your local church? It's doubtful, unless your church is very traditional. Can you guess why? It's because we've effectively brought the world into the place where God wants us to be set apart from the world.

We have done this primarily through the acceptance and use of contemporary Christian music in all its glory— through amplifiers, fancy sound systems, drum sets, electric guitars, bass guitars, and electronic pianos: through musical techniques borrowed straight from secular rock, along with the suggestive vocal techniques and body movements that come with this genre of music. While we have deceived ourselves into thinking that CCM is a way to invigorate our worship services, evangelize, and create revival, people's true hearts are revealed through statements such as, "I love that rock 'n' roll," or, "I just love to . . . rock." These are common enough statements in our secular society, but both of these statements actually came from Christian people in reference to contemporary Christian music!

As mentioned before, the term "rock 'n' roll" has been described as a sexual metaphor, and in essence, *Christians have brought the sensual/sexual into the house of the Lord and don't even realize it.*

Is this the kind of reverence for God that He desires? Can we rightly equate rock 'n' roll with a Holy God? Does God "rock"? But the effect of our acceptance of Christian rock music (an oxymoron) doesn't just end when the music is over. Its effect has resulted in an attitude shift about life in general and what is acceptable Christian behavior.

Once we let rock music into our churches, there was no stopping the limits to where it would go, and this is evidenced by the extreme behavior our Christian youth now exhibit.

As we discussed earlier in chapter four about fitting in with our culture, we have taken this way too far. So far, in fact, that the world no longer recognizes where the Church-at-large begins and where they (the world) end.

While it may be necessary to sometimes dress like those we are trying to reach, as in another completely different culture (as modesty dictates), we are *never* to dress or act in such a way that would identify ourselves with any part of society that is recognized as rebellious or questionable by the majority of the community. Yet that is exactly how segments of our Christian youth are perceived today, and the prime influence of these behaviors has been because we have placed our blessing on CCM, and by doing so, we have essentially also encouraged our youth to have lack of self-denial in other areas of their lives.

Most definitely, our choice—and our youths' choice—of music is an important factor in the process of personal sanctification. There is fruit resulting from our obedience, or lack of obedience, to God's Word regarding music, because, simply stated, *the music creates the attitude, regardless of the lyrics.* A reverential type of music (traditional hymns, Handel's *Messiah*, etc.) will encourage us to be reverent, pursue godliness, righteousness and self-control. Conversely, rap music, Christian or secular, will create a rap mind-set, and any other types of music that have evolved from jazz or rock styles will also influence the mind toward those philosophies represented by the music (punk, alternative, hip-hop, heavy-metal, reggae, etc.).

Just because something is out there in Christendom doesn't make it right. And just because something is labeled Christian doesn't necessarily mean it's biblical.

The bottom line of our acceptance of CCM is that we now have a myriad of philosophies about Christian living floating around, and the gospel, along with true, biblical Christianity, has been watered down. We have popularized the gospel, and the end result is that the Church has become secularized through the blending of the Church with the world.

Yet this blending of the Church with the world has far more serious ramifications: Because we've become so blended and so secularized, it will become harder and harder to take a stand for the Lord when the time comes for American Christians to suffer persecution, which is now so prevalent in other countries.

In other words, *because we won't have separated ourselves when times were easy, it will be very hard to take a stand when times are tough.*

There are children of Christian families today who are not familiar with the great hymns of the faith because they've never heard them in their local church. Is this sufficiently preparing them for what they will face in their lifetime when persecution comes? Which would you rather sing if you were called to face persecution? A Christian rap or rock song, an inspirational chorus sung over and over, or a hymn that has real substance and doctrine, such as "Amazing Grace" or "How Great Thou Art"?

For me, anyway, I would receive greater comfort and encouragement to stand through the messages of the hymns that have been passed down through the generations, sung by those who have been persecuted and martyred before me, and I want my children to have these hymns in their own arsenal of spiritual weapons when they need them.

But because our children—and we ourselves—won't have been firmly established in the wonderful, soul-strengthening biblical doctrines as set forth in historic hymnody, our children won't have this very effective tool for spiritual encouragement and warfare when adversity strikes.

Will our children know "Blessed Assurance, Jesus is Mine" when ridiculed for their faith or even asked or commanded to renounce their faith or the true doctrines of the Bible? Will they "stand" while recalling the wonderful words of "How Firm a Foundation," seemingly written for those suffering persecution? Will they be able to identify with the words of the hymn "Solid Rock" to help them in their hour of need, or will they fall away?[A]

How will our children stand—how can they stand—if we have taught them to compromise and blend with the world around them? They cannot stand, and will not stand, unless we train them otherwise.

The secularization of the Church has come from within itself, not from without, and the root of the problem is that the majority of Christians have decided for themselves what they will believe about music apart from God's Word, and this has affected other areas of life. We have done "what [is] right in [our] own eyes"[5]: We have failed to exercise biblical self-denial, we have failed to be diligent, we have failed to "get understanding,"[6] and it will be to the detriment of ourselves and generations to follow, should Jesus tarry.

Hosea 4:6 tells us, "My people are destroyed for lack of knowledge," and we see the evidence of this truth because we have allowed CCM to have such a pervasive hold in our lives and in our churches, with its resulting secularization of the Church.

The apostle Paul exhorts us: "And do not be conformed to this world, but be transformed by the renewing of your mind, that you may prove what is that good and acceptable and perfect will of God" (Rom. 12:2 NKJV). Making a decision to follow Jesus is only our starting point. A lifetime of pursuing holiness, of changing, growing, and becoming more and more like Jesus in all we do, is our responsibility. We should be moving toward increasing godliness, not increasing worldliness—which seems to be the general condition of Christianity in twenty-first-century America. And as we become more godly, it will be evident to others who are witnessing our transformation.

Does your life demonstrate a conformity to this world, or a transformation by the renewing of your mind through careful Bible study? Does the music you listen to testify of this transformation, or does it conform to the world's carnal music style(s)?

And if they took the music away, would you *still* follow Jesus?

Chapter Seven Notes

A. See Appendix Four for the complete lyrics to "How Firm a Foundation" and "The Solid Rock."

Chapter Eight

"If My People . . ."

*"For God shall bring every work into judgment,
. . . whether it be good, or whether it be evil."*
Ecclesiastes 12:14

O ne day, I laughingly suggested to my husband that he should have a sign in his office that read:

CHRISTIANS PAY NOW.

ALL OTHERS MAY PAY WHEN SERVICES ARE RENDERED.

Yet it's really no laughing matter. At his business, anyway, after nearly twenty-one years of law practice, the term "Christian" has almost become synonymous with "bad pay" or "no pay."

Now I don't share that scenario in order to vent. My husband doesn't have a vindictive or bitter bone in his body, and by God's grace, the Lord helps me not to, either.

But this is not the way Christians should conduct business, either in the secular world, or with Christian brothers and sisters.

It's not only in the business world that Christians are guilty of conducting themselves according to their own thinking and beliefs, however. It's within the Church, within the body of Christ, that we have tolerated, and allowed, and finally, embraced sinful behavior.

We pray for revival and quote the Scripture referred to in this chapter's title. We say we earnestly desire revival, and most discerning Christians and Christian leaders believe that we are in desperate need of true revival across this land. But as much as we say we want revival, we're ignoring an important point of Scripture, a condition that must be met before God will send revival, no matter how hard we pray.

2 Chronicles 7:14 NKJV (emphasis mine) states:

> *If my people* who are called by My name will humble themselves, and pray and seek My face, and *turn from their wicked ways, then* I will hear from heaven, and will forgive their sin and heal their land.

Another sobering verse is found in the New Testament:

> For *the time has come for judgment to begin at the house of God;* and if it begins with us first, what will be the end of those who do not obey the gospel of God?
>
> 1 Pet. 4:17 NKJV (emphasis mine)

Both of these verses refer to God's people who are not living pure lives, who need to take care of some necessary house cleaning.

It appears, though, that we believe that because we have been saved through faith by the grace of God, that our sins are forgiven and Jesus' righteousness has been accounted to us, that we are, and will be, exempt from future judgment.

Yet the judgment in these verses is not about our acceptance or rejection of Jesus Christ; it is about God dealing with His people in order to lovingly purify them for His sake. I don't know about you, but I prefer to be sensitive to obey and honor God to the best of my ability *now*; I don't want to turn a deaf ear to His gentle promptings, so that He has to send dire circumstances in order to get my attention. I already have enough challenges in everyday life to keep me on my toes, spiritually speaking.

So what are the "wicked ways" God is referring to in 2 Chronicles 7:14? Could one of them be CCM with it's sensual music techniques? I would definitely say absolutely.

I attended a church where the pastor called for serious prayer, quoting the 2 Chronicles Scripture. People went up to the altar to pray on their knees; it was a serious time of the service. The congregation was solemn, and no doubt very sincere, with heavy hearts for revival in our United States.

But later in this same service, one young woman actually stood up and began to shimmy her shoulders to the upbeat Christian music. If the music had been a traditional hymn, or even other non-carnal, God-honoring music (such as Handel's *Messiah*), would this have taken place? Does a shimmy indicate our reverence toward God?

This is not an isolated case. Clearly, we need to look to ourselves, and within our churches, and *clean up our act before we even begin to pray for our nation!*

The occurrence of flesh-pleasing music in church services across this nation is not the only example of irreverence taking place toward Holy God, though. Christian organizations who speak out against the world's sins—namely homosexuality, abortion, and divorce—are at the same time guilty of promoting and supporting the carnality of CCM within the Christian realm.

While the world can recognize and identify sensual rock music techniques and their appeal,[A] unfortunately, Christians can't, simply because we don't want to. As mentioned in chapter four, when everyone participates in and excuses CCM, it's easier to accept because we are assuaging each other's consciences. "Surely," we justify, "if that person/organization/pastor says CCM is OK, then it is OK." In short, Christians are looking for a Church-sanctioned excuse to feed the flesh and keep one foot in the world, and CCM provides it.

When we give an account to God for our deeds as Christians,[1] will such a justification be acceptable? No, because we won't be allowed "finger pointing," or excuses, before Almighty God. We will be judged only by how we obeyed God's Word, not how we reasoned or personally felt about any issue, including our Christian music.

Although we say that we seek revival to cleanse us and strengthen us for what is to come as we approach end-times and the world's increasing hatred and rejection of us, what is in fact happening as a result of the majority's acceptance of CCM, as well as its promotion and endorsement by Christian organizations, is the beginning of persecution of the Church *from within its own walls.* I have had people report to me eye-witness accounts of godly, conservative families being asked to leave their churches because these families were taking a stand for godly music, and others have had no choice but to leave their churches after having appealed to the leadership. In these cases, the discerning Christians left the church when the leadership took away the good music—music which truly modeled biblical principles for righteousness in both lyrics and style.

In other words, the worldly churches are flushing out those Christians who are trying to live godly, set apart lives—Christians who are committed to God's standards of righteousness and purity in every area. Do you think this pleases God? Frankly, it sounds to me like an end-time apostasy.[2]

Indeed, the words of 2 Timothy 3:12 ring true: ". . . all who desire to live godly in Christ Jesus will suffer persecution" (NKJV), only this time the application is from the hands of Christians toward *other* Christians. What a sad indictment for the Church!

Even otherwise godly pastors have become blinded to this issue of music in the church. Satan, who knows our weaknesses better than we ourselves do, has deceived many pastors into believing any one or more of the excuses mentioned in chapter four. Furthermore, they reason that although they may lose part of their congregation with the introduction of CCM,[B] in the end more people will come, and their church will ultimately be larger—more people to reach for Christ. But what these pastors are not realizing is that they are actually encouraging a worldly church. A church which is readily received by most of the worldly community. A church with worldly, carnal Christians, if the people are saved at all.

We must understand that CCM is accepted by the world. Its many styles please the world because the world "loves its own" and hates true, set apart believers and the godliness they are trying to live out.[3] If the world approves of what we as Christians are doing, it's most likely that we aren't "offending" them with the gospel of Christ and lives lived for Him as we should be.[4]

Contrast the world's acceptance of CCM with their distaste for traditional hymnody. This alone should reveal which music is truly godly, spiritual music, and which is a carnal imitation of the world's ungodly music.

What would the world say about the music you listen to, either privately or during corporate worship at your church? What would God say?

There should be no secular concert or event that provides music that is more pleasing to God than in His Church. It appears today, however, that if a Christian really wants to hear music that will minister to his or her soul (and experience an atmosphere of reverence and respect) one must go to a secular classical music concert or to the symphony, instead of his or her local evangelical church.

As New Testament Christians we have come full circle. As I see it, we are nearing the time that the "fullness of the Gentiles has come in."[5] We have become like the Israelites of the Old Testament: We have gone "a-whoring" after a false god—rock music. We have mixed biblical truth with false religion: Christian lyrics with sensual, pagan musical techniques.

Because we have done what is right in our own eyes,[6] we have become blinded to the sinfulness of CCM and its resulting effects in our lives. While we may think we are experiencing revival because of an exciting form of music in our churches, God has given us leanness in our souls,[7] however, we don't realize it.

Why? Although we may think that such music doesn't affect us, it really has because it has worn down our initial defenses against rock music of any kind. And as we moved to tolerance, then acceptance, of contemporary Christian music in the Church, we've taken the step into worldliness. CCM is not much different from secular rock, and the world's rock music is now also listened to and accepted by many Christians—another step has been taken. This has resulted in the slipping of our standards in other areas of life as well, especially in the entertainment arena,[c] and we no longer have true, spiritual discernment.

We've effectively stepped away from biblical Christianity regarding holiness in our lives, all because of our acceptance and love for CCM. No longer do we as Christians "hate evil" as God reminds us in His Word.[8] Instead, we embrace it. And because we so embrace the world's ways, in our music and in our entertainment choices, I question the validity of our claim that we want revival. Because true revival will only result when we as Christians return to the truth of God's written Word, rather than what *we want* God's Word to say. True revival results when Christians take seriously the Bible's admonition and God's expectation for holy living among His people. True revival results when we get serious about our own sinfulness before God and want to do something about it. We can't have it both ways—revival and sensual music techniques we wish to keep. God will not send a revival on demand and His terms in 2 Chronicles 7:14 are non-negotiable.

And so the message of both this book and my previous one is the same, whether or not we want to hear it: Contemporary Christian music *is* carnal, appeals to our carnal, fleshly self, and is wrong in the sight of God. It's a "wicked way" that has no place in the lives of God's people. It's "musical wantonness."

One day soon, God will cry, "Enough." And it won't only be the lost and sinful world that He's referring to—*it will be His people and their wicked ways.*

Will *you* have "ears to hear"?

Chapter Eight Notes

A. Refer to Endnote 15 of chapter four in which authors/book titles are listed that discuss the sensuality of rock music and the specific techniques it employs to achieve its fleshly appeal. Also see chapter three and Appendix Three.

B. Unfortunately, it's the discerning Christians who are leaving when CCM is introduced into a church.

C. For example, young children from Christian families are allowed to view R-rated movies, and movies that contain nudity, profanity, and drunkenness are now promoted among Christians.

WHERE DO WE DRAW THE LINE?

"But Samuel said, 'What then is this bleating of the sheep in my ears, and the lowing of the oxen which I hear?'"
1 Samuel 15:14 NKJV

It's been said that man-made theology indulges the flesh. It follows that what we believe about contemporary Christian music—that it is acceptable for worship, concerts, and personal listening—is a man-made theology because it, too, indulges the flesh. It is the opposite of what God has taught us throughout Scripture, as well as in the specific verses I have cited in both this book and my previous one.

Interestingly, some people who come to the Lord out of a worldly lifestyle can recognize CCM for what it truly is, flesh-pleasing music, and avoid it at all costs. They perceive the war between their carnal self—their flesh—and their new nature in Christ far better than many people who have grown up in the Church. These Christians can actually feel the magnetism of the world in such music, and discern that it pulls them away from a pure walk with the Lord. They understand that the language of the rock musical style is still rock music—Christian or otherwise—and that its effect on us doesn't contribute to our sanctification.

Those of us established in the faith should be helping and encouraging our new brothers and sisters in Christ to strive for holy living by setting an example, rather than be causing them to stumble by appealing to their flesh, only now with "Christian" music. A very naive statement that I've heard people make is that "some people should probably stay away from CCM because of their past experience with secular rock music." Yet, it's actually these people (those who have come from a worldly lifestyle) who have the discernment many Christians lack and therefore *do* stay away from CCM out of *conviction*, not due to advice from proponents of CCM.

Unfortunately, most Christians happily accept CCM as a mandate from the Church, not knowing or acknowledging that God wants us to have standards in our music, as well as in all of our life. As a result, the Church slows down the spiritual growth of believers because there are no standards regarding music in the Church, other than that the words should be spiritual.

While there are many people besides myself who are very concerned about this entire issue and its ramifications, the Church won't listen. Perhaps it's time for God to get our attention through extreme measures—suffering and/or wide-spread persecution.

In my first book, I mentioned that if the Church were to really suffer, no doubt there would be a return to our godly musical heritage.[1] This proved to be true.

Oklahoma was hit with devastating tornadoes in the spring of 1999. My family and I were traveling soon after that, and we heard on the radio that the people had sung *traditional hymns* that following Sunday after the tornado struck. They did that because those hymns give us the comfort and refuge we truly need as we seek God earnestly in times of real trial.

If you have been raised on hymns, and CCM has been introduced in your church, do you recall the initial caution you had in your spirit? Did you feel uncomfortable? Did you question the wisdom of this new music? That was the Holy Spirit telling you it wasn't right. But the Holy Spirit unheeded will give us "leanness to [our] souls."[2]

Remember, I'm not disputing innovative musical methods that are intellectually stimulating. I'm disputing flesh-pleasing, sensual music that has been brought into the Church. Neither am I debating the validity of new music that does follow biblical principles, both lyrically and musically. "New" doesn't necessarily mean "sinful."

Personally, I prefer hymns and a few traditional choruses for corporate worship, and there have been some God-honoring lyrics and beautiful musical melodies written in the past twenty years; if we simply clean them up, by removing the rock (or jazz) music techniques and vocal sensuality, they will pass biblical standards. Therefore, a mixture of both hymns and recently written (non-carnal) music would also be acceptable—and biblical—should a pastor decide it would be of benefit to his particular congregation.

As mentioned in chapter five, it's important to note that it takes a while to gain complete insight in the area of Christian music, especially if we've been listening to CCM and/or secular rock music on a regular basis. It's difficult, if not impossible, to gain discernment when we continue to participate in the thing we are trying to get discernment about. Discernment just doesn't happen. We must be willing to remove the music for a period of time before we can look at it objectively.

I discussed this in my previous book as taking a "music fast," and its importance cannot be stressed enough. Moreover, it is *essential* that we replace the old music with new music that follows traditional classical forms. As the ear gains an appreciation for a more intellectual/spiritual music, then we can finally see the difference between music that inspires the intellect, and music that appeals to the flesh.

Even if you think your particular music is OK, I would encourage you to apply a music fast also, because even some of the more seemingly innocuous CCM can still employ subtle sensuality, especially through the vocal techniques, and some very highly orchestrated hymn music has also made use of unnecessary offbeat, rock rhythms.

So to make this simple, let's put steps to this concept of a music fast.[A]

1. Remove all—repeat, *all*—CCM from your life. Also remove any influence of secular rock music as far as possible. If you watch television, have the mute button handy (and use it). To put it in Bible language, "make no provision for the flesh."[3]

2. *Actively* listen to classical music or traditional hymns. Tune your car's radio to your local classical music station.[B] Keep it there, or buy CD's from the suggested resources listed in Appendix One. Most Christian radio is not CCM-free, so if you do listen to programs, turn down the music when the station introduces a new program or during a commercial.
3. Continue this music fast vigilantly for at least thirty days.

Musical taste is as much an acquired taste as our taste for food. If we lived in certain parts of Mexico, for example, our diets would consist of fried worms and crickets, among other things. We, as Americans, would say "yuck," but the Mexicans say "yum!" (Some of these insects are actually considered delicacies.)

I recently read that it takes about ten tastings of a new food until kids will like it. Similarly, we must consciously make the effort to listen to music that follows biblical principles, because what we are doing is training our ears to discern the differences between carnal and non-carnal music. It's the same as "renewing our minds,"[4] only in this instance, we're renewing it with good music.

Musical discernment will not come if we don't actively pursue it, or if we approach the music fast with the attitude of, "Well, OK, but I'm going back to my CCM when it's over." We must really be seeking God's heart on this issue, with our own hearts ready and willing to obey.

I know a music fast works because I have had first-hand reports, as well as my own experience, that it really helped people to gain insight and discernment.

When you end your music fast, listen to a CCM song for contrast. Notice several things:

1. The vocalist's technique. Is it breathy, gravelly, and/or sliding around the notes? Is it sultry? Would you want your spouse or significant other to be talked to in this tone of voice?
2. How does the overall music make you want to move?[C] Are you responding to the melody, or to an additional drum beat? (Drums don't have to be the only indicator here; strong, or even subtle, offbeat carnal rhythms in a melody can also cause carnal body reactions.)
3. Do you get a sense of purity, as with traditional hymns? Or does it sound worldly?
4. Are you aware of a certain pull toward worldliness that this music conveys?
5. Finally, if you were to stand before the Lord face-to-face and sing in this musical style, would your conscience be completely and absolutely clear?[D]

The question may arise, "Where do we draw the line?" In my first book, I explained that it must be drawn at no repetitious second and fourth offbeat drum rhythms[E] (and/or other sultry techniques, by way of vocals or instrumentation, as in jazz music). Even though some music that contains these rhythms and/or techniques may not necessarily cause us to move in a carnal manner, the fact remains that these are sensual techniques, and discernment of these comes only after a period of time of applying biblical principles and listening to a high standard of music.

Furthermore, many of the earlier forms of CCM (which appear innocent by today's standards) are exactly like earlier forms of rock music, which was called lewd, vulgar, and "dirty music" from its inception, but now even Christians laugh at rock music's beginnings. What we don't realize, though, is that we, too, have bought into the sexual revolution, which was reflected and encouraged by rock music as it developed.

How so? Because what should be blatant to us (rock music's beat, which appeals to our carnal self) now seems innocuous and acceptable. Yet while we may have moved *our* "line" for acceptable music, God didn't move His. As stated previously, our desensitization to sensual music doesn't make it OK in God's eyes.

CCM is a Trojan horse within Christianity. And much like the Trojan horse that led to the downfall of ancient Troy, or even a "trojan" inside your computer, the Trojan horse of CCM has been designed to destroy biblical Christianity. Satan knew that Christians would not accept the rebellious and sinful lyrics of rock music, but he knew that after having been exposed to it in the secular world, we would eventually accept its flesh-appealing rhythms that break down our inhibitions. With secular society's acceptance of secular rock music, it also accepted rock music's agenda for sexual revolution and liberalism. Christians are targeted with the same agenda, and it's working.

Early CCM (Jesus music) was patterned after early rock music, and that's the subtle beginning of where we are today. If we don't draw a line at any and all repetitive offbeat rhythms, we'll become desensitized to those little offbeats (accept them as OK) and then continue to move our line. Once again we'll have given ourselves over to our flesh, rather than have taken a stand to deny our flesh. If we adhere to high standards for music, however, over time we will perceive that even the small, offbeat drum rhythms are subtle, sensual appeals to our carnal, fleshly self.

The point is not how close we can come to a line we draw for ourselves regarding acceptable music; the goal is how close we can come to God's standards revealed through Scripture so that we may obey and please Him in our musical choices. We should be willing to give up our rights to all of our music. And the end result is that we will be blessed in our hearts because of our obedience.

Now you have a choice to make, and it's not an easy one: Keep your CCM, or discard it in its entirety. I know it is a difficult decision, especially because of the monetary investment that has been made. But if you had pornography in your house and were convicted about that, would you keep it? `

If, however, you allow yourself to return to CCM, or only listen to selected pieces, you will start to excuse it and rationalize it all over again and you will lose your discernment; you will have "made provision for the flesh." As with any area of life, we must constantly be on guard.

What if you are convinced as a parent, but your teenagers aren't? As a parent of a teenager myself, I feel I can offer some practical advice.

Did it ever occur to you that God is more interested in your child's soul, in his or her sanctification, than even you are? When I realized this, I relaxed. That doesn't mean that I quit my parental duties and responsibilities, but it does mean that I can now pray with more confidence that God will work in my children's lives, regardless of how I might personally mess up.

I also realized that if God gave *me* certain convictions, He could give my children biblical convictions, as well. God, indeed, is our "partner in parenting."

Do you remember the apostle Paul stating basically that he didn't want to covet until the Law told him not to?[5] The same principle applies to us, as well as to our children. Who among us hasn't seen a Wet Paint sign, yet wanted to touch the paint to see if it really was wet? It's only through God's grace and the power of the Holy Spirit that we develop convictions and want to obey Him out of love.

But as soon as we tell most kids, "Thou shalt not . . .," they'll want to do whatever we are warning them against. It's human nature. So my first suggestion is to not be dictatorial about your teen's music. And here are some positive things you can do to guide your children.[F]

1. If you've personally had a change of heart regarding CCM, tell them and tell them *why*.
2. Challenge them to read my books. Encourage them to go on a music fast.
3. In the common areas of your home and in your car, play God-honoring music so that they can begin to become accustomed to hearing it. Don't assume they don't or won't like classical music. If they're listening to CCM, no doubt they've also attended movies such as *Star Wars*, which had some excellent "classical" music. Did they complain?[G]
4. Explain the difference between music that appeals to our carnal, fleshly self and music that inspires the spiritual/intellectual. To further illustrate the point, give them the movement test outlined in chapter one of this book, using some of their upbeat CCM, contrasted

to traditional hymns and/or classical music. Ask them if they are responding to a simple, straight-forward melody, or to the drums or other offbeat rhythms that cause carnal body movements.

5. Buy them some new music that truly honors God. Get a variety of good styles so that they can discover some they might personally like.[H]

6. Always maintain your sense of humor. My husband and I have found that this goes a long way toward keeping communication channels open with kids.

7. Pray: 1) that God will capture their hearts, convict them, and show them the truth, 2) that they will be sensitive to the Holy Spirit, 3) that God will show *you* what you can do to turn their hearts toward Him. Because if we can truly get our teen's hearts for the Lord, the rest will follow.[1] (Outward compliance doesn't guarantee inward change of heart.)

8. Finally, remember our goal as parents is to get them to recognize their accountability to God in everything they do. (At times, I've been known to tell my kids, "It's between you and the Lord.")

If your children are younger, obviously you can begin their musical discernment training earlier. Provide classical music and traditional hymns at appropriate times during the day, and possibly as they go to bed. You can actively instruct them in right and wrong regarding acceptable music because they are more teachable. And don't forget to help them memorize the words to some of the great hymns.[J]

In this book, as well as in my previous one, I have purposely chosen not to name specific CCM artists or songs.

The reason I have done this is that I want people to learn to discern all types of music for themselves. And if I had named names and/or titles, people could get around that by choosing to listen to those I did not name. Moreover, the tendency for all of us is to want instant discernment. It doesn't work that way.

For an insight to be our own, we have to obey God and make applications to our life as the Lord shows us; musical discernment does not happen overnight. That is exactly why those who defend CCM cannot hear anything wrong: They're desensitized to the level of rock music they are listening to, as well as anything up to their particular level on the rock music tolerance scale. And until a person is truly willing to take a music fast, and is truly willing to seek God's will and obey Him (no matter what), there will be no real musical discernment, there will be no understanding. Period.

Yes, there should be lyrical discernment because these are obvious. But other than the initial differences in body responses that I've pointed out, the subtleties of further musical discernment take longer to develop. Discernment with our bodies is only the first step; the ear and the spirit also have to be trained. We *must* learn to listen spiritually, because even some technically correct music may still be spiritually "dark." And as a side benefit of learning musical discernment, we gain spiritual insights in other areas of life as well because our spirits will become more sensitive.

God does want us to have discernment in our lives, in music as well as all other areas, and He has called us to a life of separateness from the world[7] so that we can gain discernment and live our lives in a manner pleasing to Him—so that we can become like Christ. And the more we become like Christ, the more we will understand and see that CCM does not conform to biblical standards. A life of separateness doesn't necessarily mean that we pull apart from our culture, rather it means that while we are in our present culture, we walk worthy of the Lord and according to His Word, so that others may see a true difference and freshness in our lives and want it for themselves.

The Christian life lived for God will involve some active and sometimes difficult, if not painful, choices as we say no to our flesh, and no to activities in our culture which would not be pleasing to the Lord. Separate is *not* synonymous with puritanical, however, because Christians do have the freedom to enjoy things in life so long as the activity is not contrary to Scripture or scriptural principles, or cause us, or others, to sin. (For example, sports, mini-golf, certain hobbies, or a theme park.)

While we may be passively exposed to worldly music at these events, our responsibility is that we do not search them out for the worldly music, or for other things that we might encounter that would not please our Savior. We remain separate in our behavior, yet we remain "in this present world."[8]

There is no way we can witness to a lost and dying world if we sequester ourselves off in the middle of nowhere. But neither can we expect to truly reach others for Christ if we are behaving just like the world.

Yet, we can witness through set apart music, just as we can witness through a set apart life. In fact, set apart music is a vital part of a set apart life because not only does it witness of a completely changed life, it helps us as Christians to fulfill our obligation to live a separated life. CCM, however, cannot witness of a completely changed life because it is not truly set apart music according to

God's standards, simply because of its appeal to the flesh. Recall 1 John 2:16: "For all that is in the world, *the lust of the flesh,* and the lust of the eyes, and the pride of life, *is not of the Father, but is of the world*" (emphasis mine).

Therefore, to hold to the biblical standard of "spiritual songs" in its truest application in our choice of music, even in today's society, is not in any way puritanical. It's simply biblical. But because our society is so increasingly sinful, if we do hold to the high standard in music that God wants for our worship of Him and in our lives lived for Christ, there will be an increasingly wide gap between the world's ways and true, biblical Christianity. There should be.

Unfortunately, the Church has become so worldly that the gap is now only a tiny sliver of light, and then only on issues such as abortion and homosexuality. And sadly, this light is closing in some areas of Christendom, as well.

The Christian path has become wider and wider as history has unfolded, but the words of Jesus in Matthew 7:13–14 still apply to all those who seek a path to Heaven. Not only is the way to Heaven difficult and narrow, but so is the Christian life lived out in obedience to Him. Still, it is a joyful life, willingly lived out of love for our precious Savior, because we have been redeemed.

Undoubtedly, contemporary Christian music is a "broad way" among religious circles, a way that is leading many people into thinking they're OK with the Lord, when in reality they aren't. It's a musical method that we've allowed our deceitful hearts[9] to highly esteem. But God, Who knows our hearts, has told us in His Word that, ". . . what is highly esteemed among men is an abomination in the sight of God" (Luke 16:15 NKJV).

Does your heart "highly esteem" music which contains identifiable, sensual techniques, or does your heart "hunger and thirst after righteousness,"[10] even in your music? Do others see your life becoming increasingly holy, increasingly set apart to the Lord? And if they took the music away, would you still follow Jesus?

This book has necessarily been a hard saying, but my ultimate goal, my ultimate message, is one of encouraging the Church toward holiness, both individually and corporately. I sincerely hope you now understand that CCM, with its sensual vocals and flesh-appealing techniques, does not fulfill righteousness for Christian music.

In the introduction of this book, I stated that there will be three categories of readers: those who "have ears to hear," those who will be angry, and those who will be indifferent.

Indifference indicates complacency, much like the lukewarm Christians God speaks about in Revelation.[11] It could also indicate a lack of true salvation. Defensiveness or anger, because our toes have been stepped on, indicates that the message has hit the mark. Have you ever heard the statement, "The truth only hurts when it ought to"? This is not to be confused with righteous indignation, which is only rightly defined as a righteous hatred of things that are evil.

But the heart of one who seeks the truth will ponder the things in this book, search the whole counsel of Scripture, and prayerfully consider God's will concerning music in his or her life; this one will "have ears to hear." And the fact is that the closer we walk with the Lord, the more we *will* desire holiness in our life. We will increasingly recognize subtle things in our lives that we once thought were OK, but now we understand differently.

This is why it is so important that we give music serious consideration, because the music we listen to plays a key role in our sanctification and in our spiritual discernment.

What will your response be? Won't you ask God to give you wisdom and to change your heart, if necessary? More than anything, God wants us to be conformed to the image of His Son.

> For we must all appear before the judgment seat of Christ, that each one may receive the things done in the body, according to what he has done, whether good or bad. 2 Cor. 5:10 NKJV

What will that day be like for you? When God reviews the music that you listened to privately or promoted in church, will you be rewarded for obeying His Word, or will you stand ashamed before Him to hear those identifiable, sensual techniques which could easily have been eliminated from Christian music?

It is my heartfelt prayer that you will be able to stand before the Lord with no regrets, no sorrow, that you did not heed God's Word in the area of music, and that you will hear those wonderful words that will be a balm to our world-tossed souls: "Well done, good and faithful servant . . . Enter into the joy of your lord."[12]

Let those who have ears to hear, hear.

Chapter Nine Notes

A. A music fast is profitable for any type of music we have questions about. Remove the music for a period of time and use traditional hymns and/or classical music as the standard.

B. If the classical station is airing a jazz, swing, or big band program, avoid those, too.

C. Review chapters one and three for the specific differences in movement each type of music elicits. Also refer to Appendix Three for carnal techniques used in music.

D. See Appendix Five for further questions to answer about CCM.

E. Or any other repetitious drum (or other rhythm instrument) pattern that doesn't support the melody or dominate it. NOTE: Because the drums in traditional march music support—but don't dominate—the melody, with the heaviest accents always on the first beat, traditional march music is fine.

F. These suggestions are for youth/teens who are open to pleasing the Lord. Truly rebellious teens may need professional help. My first book, however, has been recommended as a resource to help families with troubled teens discern what would be appropriate music for their home.[6] Concerning rebellion, I suggest the pamphlet, "Preventing and Turning Rebellion in Youth." See Appendix One, "Books/Booklets."

G. No, our family did not see this movie; however, we did review the soundtrack. While there are a few good musical works on this recording, there are also a few strange sounding pieces, so I can't in good conscience recommend it.

H. See Appendix One for further resources to help your family learn how to truly discern music.

I. An excellent resource for addressing a child's (or teen's) heart is the book, *Shepherding a Child's Heart*, by Tedd Tripp. See Appendix One, "Books/Booklets."

J. See Appendix One and Appendix Four.

RESOURCES

MUSICAL STYLES WITHIN BIBLICAL PARAMETERS

The following list begins to demonstrate the vast array of musical styles which follow biblical principles for our music. Within these parameters, we are free to exercise our personal preferences. Of course, even within these parameters, common sense should prevail when choosing music for worship, rather than for personal enjoyment and entertainment.

Secular
1. Traditional folk music. This includes ethnic music such as Irish, Scottish, German, Slovak, Greek, etc.
2. Barbershop quartet
3. Marches (traditional)
4. Waltzes
5. Opera (It should also be morally upright in the lyrical content.)

6. Classical, which covers a span of over 1800 years and provides us with broad range of styles: Baroque, Classical, Romantic, and Contemporary, etc.
7. Selected contemporarily written music, such as from motion picture soundtracks. (*The Sound of Music*; *Chitty-Chitty, Bang-Bang*; *Anne of Green Gables*, etc.)

Sacred
1. Traditional four-part gospel music
2. Traditional hymns and choruses
3. Biblical oratorios, i.e., Handel's *Messiah*
4. Biblical cantatas, i.e., Bach's *A Mighty Fortress Is Our God*
5. Gregorian Chant
6. Contemporarily written music which follows biblical principles (not most CCM).

These are only a few suggestions to get you started in the area of musical discernment. I would also recommend that you get catalogs from the sources listed on page 177 and choose from those, too.

Movie Soundtracks
Not all movie soundtracks completely pass biblical standards for music, and some walk-out music is extremely sensual/carnal. There are, however, a couple worth mentioning. My suggestions here do not necessarily endorse the movies (but I would never suggest any movie soundtrack from an immoral movie, even though the music was perfect).

I think that the music on these two soundtracks will provide a wholesome and righteous bridge from CCM/secular rock to classical music and traditional hymnody, while at the same time provide training for the ears and spirit in musical discernment.

In short, the music on these soundtracks follows biblical principles. They are available at secular music stores, although they might have to be special ordered.

- GLORY. A Civil War movie. The Harlem Boys' Choir sings on a couple of songs. Listen for the call of a distant bugle on track two. Tracks four and eight are military marches; track nine depicts a battle. (Produced by James Horner. Tri-Star Pictures, Inc., 1989.)
- GETTYSBURG. Another Civil War epic, and the musical selections range from exhilarating and noble to poignant. This is one of our family's favorite secular CD's. (Music by Randy Edelman. Turner Pictures, Inc., BMG Music, 1993.)

CLASSICAL MUSIC

"Why is secular classical music OK, even if it's written by an atheist?" you might ask.

Most classical music follows the principles of Scripture; it's intellectual, pure music that doesn't appeal to our lower, carnal self. Additionally, the early composers of the broad category we call classical understood that, ultimately, music was to direct our attention to the Creator, and they endeavored to do this through their compositions. Therefore, as each era has built upon the foundation that the early composers laid, most forms of classical music follow biblical principles. (Recall that Western civilization music began in the New Testament Church.)[A]

Not one person can accurately say that he or she doesn't like classical music, because it's doubtful that anyone has heard every piece of classical music ever written. There are different styles within the classical music realm, and even different styles and nuances from composer to composer.

The following are just a few selections from differing historical periods of music. It's also a good idea to get CD's (or cassettes) that offer "The Best of" a particular composer or period of music (i.e. Baroque, Romantic, Classical, etc.); these will introduce you to a composer or musical era through the most popular works of either the composer or the particular time of musical history. Some of the selections I've listed are very familiar to us because we have heard parts of them in movies or television programs.

Baroque Period (1600–1750)

BACH, J.S.
- *Toccata and Fugue in D Minor* This is the dramatic organ composition most all of us have heard.
- "Jesu, Joy of Man's Desiring" from *Cantata No. 147*
- "Air on the G String" This is commonly played on the guitar and is a bit melancholy, but very beautiful.
- "Prelude in E Major" from *Suite No. 4 for Lute* Very quick and lively.
- *Brandenburg Concertos* There are six and all are very energetic (not boring).

HANDEL
- *Messiah*
- *Water Music*
- *Royal Fireworks Music* Both *Water Music* and *Royal Fireworks Music* are exceptionally dynamic.

PACHELBEL
- *Canon in D Major* We hear this at weddings; it's elegant.

VIVALDI
- *Mandolin Concerto* Very "happy."
- *The Four Seasons* This is a good mix of both gentle and lively music, and captures the essence of each season.

Classical Period (c. 1750–1815)

BEETHOVEN
- *Piano Sonata No. 14* ("Moonlight Sonata")
- *Symphony No. 6* ("Pastoral") The music portrays singing birds and thunderstorms.
- *Symphony No. 9* ("Choral") Includes "Ode to Joy" (which has been adapted to our hymns, "Alleluia! Alleluia!" and "Joyful, Joyful, We Adore Thee").

HAYDN, FRANZ JOSEPH
- *Trumpet Concerto in E-Flat Major*
- *Symphony No. 104* ("London")

MOZART, WOLFGANG AMADEUS
- *Clarinet Quintet in A*
- *String Quartet No. 17 in B-Flat Major* ("Hunt")
- *Piano Concerto No. 20*
- *Serenade in G Major* ("Eine Kleine Nachtmusik")

Romantic Period (c. 1815–1910)

CHOPIN
- *Nocturne in E-Flat Major*, Opus 9, No. 2 Very lyrical. All of his nocturnes are excellent.
- *Douze Etudes* Opus 25, No. 1
- *Piano Concerto No. 2 in F Minor*
- Waltz, Opus 64, No. 1 ("Minute Waltz")

ROSSINI
- *William Tell Overture* This is *The Lone Ranger* theme song from the early '60's television program.

STRAUSS, JOHANN
- Waltzes, i.e., "Blue Danube," "Emperor"

TCHAIKOVSKY
- *Swan Lake*
- *1812 Overture* Musically illustrates a war.
- *The Nutcracker Suite*
- *Piano Concerto No. 1*

Some of the other composers of this period include: Liszt, Debussy, Verdi, Schubert, Mendelssohn, Brahms, Grieg, Schumann.

Contemporary Period (twentieth century: c. 1910–present)[B]

ANDERSON, LEROY
- *The Typewriter* This has an actual typewriter "playing" along with the orchestra, complete with the bell at the end of a line. It is very cute.

- *The Syncopated Clock* Another fun piece. Mr. Anderson's music is classified as "light instrumental," and he has done many similar works. Look for them under Boston Pops or St. Louis Symphony recordings.

RACHMANINOFF
- *Piano Concerto No. 2* A most outstanding piece of music.
- *Prelude in C-Sharp Minor*, Opus 3, No. 2 Another great work for the piano.
- *Rhapsody on a Theme of Paganini* This is gorgeous.

SOUSA
- Marches, i.e., "Stars and Stripes Forever," "Washington Post"

(NOTE: Both Rachmaninoff and Sousa overlap the Romantic and Contemporary periods.)

There are also many more notable contemporary composers—Stravinsky, Shostakovich, Khachaturian, Walton, etc. In this period, some composers move into abstract types of music, much like other abstract art (paintings, sculptures, etc.). Therefore, when selecting new music, we should be very careful to listen to the Holy Spirit and test all music against biblical principles for righteousness and orderliness. (Does it appeal to the flesh? Does it have a beginning, middle, and ending? Does it make sense? Some classical pieces do appeal to our flesh, and some contain spiritual darkness. Developing spiritual discernment is essential.)

RECORDINGS

Classical Music

The following are a few collections which contain several of the above mentioned selections, and one different type of album.

• *Classical Occasions: Sunday.* Includes Beethoven's "Pastoral" Symphony and a clarinet concerto by Mozart. (Joysong Music, Barbour Publishing, Inc.: Classic Fox Records, 1998.)

• *Classical Occasions: Friends.* Light background music. Tchaikovsky's "Song Without Words," Vivaldi's "Winter," and many more selections from composers such as Haydn, Chopin, Mozart, and Grieg. (Joysong Music, Barbour Publishing, Inc.: Classic Fox Records, 1998.)

• *The Best of Baroque. Canon in D* by Pachelbel, Vivaldi's "Summer" from *The Four Seasons*, and *Toccata and Fugue in D Minor* by Bach are a few of the selections on this album. (SPJ Music, Inc.: Copyright, 1999.)

• *Early American Collection,* by Miller-Rowe Consort. This is a delightful and refreshing recording which features hammer dulcimer and classical guitar. Includes early American tunes such as "Ash Grove," "Froggie Went A'Courtin'," "The Water is Wide," and eleven more recordings, some Celtic. (Michael M. Miller and David L. Rowe: Copyright, 1994.) Miller-Rowe Music, PO Box 683, Spartanburg, SC 29304-0683. A website is also available to hear snippets from their other albums: www.miller-rowe.com.

Sacred Music

NOTE: There are a lot of styles of hymns available now. And while some are advertised as traditional, many contain rock rhythms in the background, sensual vocals, or even use some modified jazz styles of music. Be very careful, or only order music from the resources I've listed below.

Choral

• *Rise Up, O Men of God*, by the ALERT Men's Choir with full orchestra. This recording includes "Battle Hymn of the Republic," "God Bless America," "Amazing Grace," and more. Available through Discover Christian Music (see "Resources for Sacred Music" on page 177).

• *Psalms and Spiritual Songs for Meditation,* by Jeff Barth. Gentle melodies with guitar accompaniment. A good way to memorize some of the Psalms, as well as Matthew 5:1–10 and 1 Thessalonians 4:13–18. Parable Publishing House, 339 Parkhill Road, Cornwall, VT 05753. Or call 1-802-462-2001.

• *Sing to the Lord*, duets and solos by Tim and Deborah Fisher, with beautiful orchestrations. "Sing to the Lord," "Love Lifted Me," "My Heavenly Father," "Great is Thy Faithfulness," and many more. Available through Sacred Music Services (see "Resources for Sacred Music").

NOTE: For more choral selections, obtain catalogs from companies listed under "Resources for Sacred Music."

Instrumental

• *Classical Hymns.* These are wonderful and relaxing, featuring classical guitar, violins, viola, and cello. "Simple Gifts," "Praise God, From Whom all Blessings Flow," "Joyful, Joyful We Adore Thee," and twelve more hymns. (Produced by John Mock. Green Hill Productions, Nashville, TN, 1995.)

• *Moments with the Savior.* (From the creators of *Hymnworks* and *Symphony of Praise.*) Linda McKechnie (piano) and the London Festival Orchestra are featured on this recording conducted by Don Marsh. "Shine, Jesus, Shine," "He Hideth My Soul," "There Is a Redeemer," "The Lord's Prayer," several hymn medleys, and more hymns are all nicely arranged and performed. Includes a devotional CD. (Produced by Don Marsh. Brentwood Records, 1999.)

• *It Is Well with My Soul.* Inspirational Harp Solos by Joe Barth. Selections on this beautiful recording include "Amazing Grace," "Just as I Am," "It Is Well with My Soul," and a few hymn medleys, such as "O Sacred Head, Now Wounded" and "When I Survey the Wondrous Cross." Available on cassette or CD. Contact Parable Publishing House, 339 Parkhill Road, Cornwall, VT 05753. 1-802-462-2001.

• *Hymns in Brass.* (Vol. I) "Stand Up, Stand Up for Jesus," "We're Marching to Zion," "Praise to the Lord, the Almighty." Fifteen selections in all. Sacred Music Services.

Children

• *Kamp Kids Sing His Praise.* Orchestra by Mac Lynch. "All Creatures of Our God and King," "Sing Glory," "Savior Like a Shepherd Lead Us," and more. Discover Christian Music.

• *The Wise Man Built His House.* This is a story/music recording with one side split-trax for sing-along. Songs include, "Trust and Obey," "I'll be a Sunbeam." Sacred Music Services.

• *Patch the Pirate Adventures.* Character qualities and biblical principals are taught through adventure stories and songs. A variety of titles are available through Majesty Music.

(Addresses for each of the above companies are listed on page 177.)

Resources for Sacred Music

The following companies can be completely trusted as sources for godly Christian music. Call or write for catalogs.

Majesty Music
PO Box 6524
Greenville, SC 29606
1-800-334-1071

Majesty Music not only offers musical recordings, but they have holiday cantatas for SATB, workbooks to help congregational accompanists, and collections for smaller choirs, as well as other musical helps for churches.

The "Patch the Pirate" adventure series for children teaches biblical values with cute stories and music. Choral books are available in this series to aid churches that have children's ministries develop a Patch the Pirate Club.

Discover Christian Music
519 Piedmont Golf Course Road
Piedmont, SC 29673
1-888-414-4326

Discover Christian Music has a very large selection of good, sacred music.

Sacred Music Services
PO Box 17072
Greenville, SC 29606
1-800-767-4326
www.smsrecordings.com.

As well as providing a variety of fine recordings that include children's choirs, brass choirs, and orchestra, SMS has hymn story dramatizations. You can listen to excerpts from some of their recordings on their website.

Other Resources

Books/Booklets
• "Examine Yourself," a small booklet by Pastor John MacArthur that helps the reader to discern whether or not he or she is a true believer/follower of Jesus Christ, according to the Bible. It may be obtained by contacting their office at 1-800-55GRACE. Or write to: Grace to You, PO Box 4000, Panorama City, CA 91412-4000. On the Web: www.gty.org.
• "Preventing and Turning Rebellion in Youth," by Jeff Barth. A very insightful and helpful pamphlet/article. Parable Publishing House, 339 Parkhill Road, Cornwall, VT 05753. 1-802-462-2001.
• *Shepherding a Child's Heart*, by Tedd Tripp (Wapwallopen, PA: Shepherd Press, 1995). Offers practical, biblical steps for reaching your child's heart in matters of discipline, communication, and character development. Video and audio tape series are also available. Shepherding the Heart Ministries, 1-888-251-1619.
• *Harmony at Home... Straight answers to help you build healthy music standards,* by Tim Fisher (Greenville, SC: Sacred Music Services, 1999). The first half of this book discusses how to develop a godly musical foundation for your family. The second half answers twenty questions such as: If someone has a good testimony and people are getting saved, how can you criticize them? What about Country Western,

Southern Gospel, and Blue Grass music? Why can't Christian teenagers have their own music? What about praise and worship music?

This book also has an excellent "Tools" chapter in which the author suggests hymnals and chorus books, hymn study books, biographies of some of the great hymn writers, books on the history of hymnology, as well as books for further reading about CCM, secular rock music, and church music philosophy. It also includes a guide to basic classical music selections for both adults and children. Highly recommended! Available through Sacred Music Services.

• *Measuring the Music,* by John Makujina (Salem, OH: Schmul Publishing Co., 2000). A very systematic, very scholarly, evaluation of contemporary Christian music. Available through Sacred Music Services.

• *Oh, Be Careful Little Ears—Contemporary Christian Music . . . Is That in the Bible?* by Kimberly Smith with Lee Smith (Enumclaw, WA: WinePress Publishing, 1997). Researches contemporary Christian music both historically and biblically. Includes information about New Age music and pop music. Available through WinePress Publishing. Ordering information at the back of this book.

Tapes and Videos

• *How to Evaluate Music,* by Pastor T.P. Johnston (audio cassette, 1999). This is an outstanding, two-tape set from a seminar on understanding music from a biblical perspective. Pastor Johnston plays musical clips to aid in discernment and gives a very understandable explanation of music. Also includes a recording of actual music transcribed from notations on Hebrew manuscripts of the Psalms. Highly recommended! Video also available. Contact: Institute in

Basic Life Principles, Box One, Oak Brook, IL 60522-3001. 1-800-323-9610, or 1-800-323-9800.

• *Sound Understanding Music Conference*: Fall, 1999, by Pastor T.P. Johnston, with Dr. Al Smith. An eight-session, in-depth seminar, available on both audio and video tapes. Contact: Don Currin Ministries, 4675 Dawsonville Highway, Gainesville, GA 30506. 1-770-781-8080.

• *Praise Him in Joyful Song,* by Tim Fisher and Pastor Danny Sweatt (Greenville, SC: Sacred Music Services, 1990). This audio cassette series includes discussions with various pastors and music leaders from across the country as well as personal testimonies. Subjects discussed: Building a philosophy of Christian music, music in the home, church music, music and culture, contemporary Christian music, and questions and answers. Available through Sacred Music Services.

• *The Language of Music,* by Dr. Frank Garlock (Greenville, SC: Majesty Music, 1992). A six-tape video series seminar that would be great as part of a church-wide music discernment program. Titles include: "The God of Music," "The Message of Music," "The Sound of Music," "The Gospel of Music," "The Effects of Music," "The Purpose of Music."

This series provides musical examples to aid in discernment, as well as enlightening quotes about music from both secular and non-secular sources. Dr. Garlock did his graduate work at Eastman School of Music and has taught biblical principles for music all around the world. Available through Majesty Music at 1-800-334-1071.

• *What's Wrong with Christian Rock?* by Jeff Godwin (Bloomington, IN: The Rock Ministries, 1992). NOTE: This video is not suitable for young children because it contains some explicit material.

Many other video and audio tape resources and seminar messages concerning both secular and Christian rock music are also available through Jeff Godwin's ministry. Probably more than any other person or ministry today, Jeff has intensely researched the connection between demons and rock music and gives seminars on this topic.

For more information about further resources or to schedule a seminar, contact:

THE ROCK MINISTRIES
PO BOX 2181
BLOOMINGTON, IN 47402
1-812-834-5267

Appendix One Notes

A. Refer to *Oh, Be Careful Little Ears* for a brief historical overview of classical music and hymns.

B. For lack of a better term, "Contemporary Period" includes many styles of music that have been composed and categorized during the twentieth century: Expressionism, Impressionism, Neoclassical, Modern, Abstract, Nonobjective, etc.

CHRISTIAN MUSIC COMPARISON CHART

Contemporary Christian (*offbeat or jazz rhythms, etc.*)	Godly Christian (*straight-forward rhythms*)
1. Disorderly. (1 Cor. 14:33)	1. Orderly. (1 Cor. 14:40)
2. Rhythms originated from pagan culture. (Jer. 10:2a; Rom. 8:7)	2. Religious music of Western civilization originated in New Testament church. (Eph. 5:19; Col. 3:16)
3. Appeals to the flesh. (Rom. 8:5a, 8:8)	3. Appeals to the spirit. (John 4:23–24; Rom. 8:6b)
4. Pictures conflict of our spirit with our flesh. (Rom. 7:14–25; Gal. 5:17)	4. Pure; pictures denial of flesh and self-control. (Rom. 8:12–14; Gal. 5:22–25; Tit. 2:11-12)

5. Tickles the ears to draw people to the church. (2 Tim. 4:3)	5. Acknowledges that it is God Who draws people to Christ through the Holy Spirit. (John 6:44)
6. Imitation of the world. (1 John 2:15; Luke 16:15b)	6. Separateness from the world. (Rom. 12:2; 2 Cor. 6:14–17)
7. Use of sensual techniques. (1 John 2:16)	7. No such techniques used. Morally righteous. (Rom. 13:14; 1 Pet. 1:15–16)
8. Contributes to emotionalism in worship. (John 4:23–24; 1 Cor. 14:33)	8. Encourages true, spirit-filled worship. (John 4:23–24; Phil. 3:3)

Scripture references are not exhaustive (2 Tim. 3:16–17).

CARNAL (SENSUAL) MUSIC TECHNIQUES

This appendix is to be used as a starting point for identifying and discerning sensual elements in music. New techniques may be developed, but they all will be able to be evaluated by asking ourselves, "How is this music affecting my body?" Do we merely want to tap our toes along with the *melody's* rhythm, perhaps even think of a folk-type dance or march (good music)? Or, does our body want to respond with a thrust of the head, shoulder, or hip? (This response could either be to an additional drum rhythm, a "teasing" rhythm, or even a strong, offbeat rhythm of a melody.) Does the music create a subtle, sensual sound, with or without causing a carnal body response? Each of these are indications that the music is appealing to the flesh, and is therefore carnal.

1. *Offbeat accents.* These are accents, usually on the second and fourth beats, which are unrelated to the melody

and may be either subtle (quiet), or driving (loud and forceful). They will be continuous throughout a portion of the music, or throughout the entire piece, always played by a drum, bass guitar, or other rhythm or percussive instrument. This is the classic rock musical style.

2. *Any rhythm which conflicts with the melody.* The melody should always be priority, with no drum, or other instrument, playing a rhythm that conflicts with it or dominates the music.

3. *Swing rhythms.* These evoke a sense, or feeling, of "da, dah, da, dah, dah." (The big-band sound.) Also, any rhythm or melody in which beats seem to be held slightly longer than necessary (teasing) such as, boogie woogie, jazz, "cool," etc.

4. *An offbeat rhythm that has no melody.* Usually solely drums, sometimes with cymbals or other percussive devices added. This is a strong, rhythmic piece of music that evokes carnal body movements.

5. *Melodies that are obviously based on strong, repetitive, offbeat rhythm patterns.* These can be played by a single instrument or an entire band. Some examples include calypso or reggae music and strong jazz or rock music. These types of "rhythm melodies" also cause the body (torso) to respond in carnal movements.

6. *Sliding or scooping.* Used mainly by vocalists and jazz musicians. This technique is achieved by sliding down from one note to a lower note, or scooping up from a lower note to a higher note. The slide or scoop can pass through any number of notes between the starting note and the ending note. For example, the scoop could go from one

note to the note next to it on the musical scale, or, it could go an entire octave (eight notes) or more. Also included in this technique is the practice of landing briefly on the note just below what is written in the music, and then scooping up to the intended note.

Note: A similar musical technique used in operatic (and classical) music is called a *glissando;* however, because the operatic vocalist makes a (brief) distinction of each note that is passed over, the *glissando* isn't sensual.

7. *Breathiness or gravelliness.* Used by vocalists.

8. *Sensual vibrato.* Vibrato is slight fluctuation in pitch of a note being held for any length of time. It becomes sensual when the fluctuation is slowed. Used by vocalists and jazz musicians.

9. *Dissonances.* Tense, unresolved sounding chords or other techniques that are grating to the ears.

Appendix Four

HOW FIRM A FOUNDATION

Words: Rippon's *Selection of Hymns*, 1787
Music: Traditional American melody

1. How firm a foundation, ye saints of the Lord,
   Is laid for your faith in His excellent Word!
   What more can He say than to you He hath said,
   To you who for refuge to Jesus have fled?

2. "Fear not, I am with thee; O be not dismayed,
   For I am thy God, and will still give thee aid;
   I'll strengthen thee, help thee, and cause thee to stand,
   Upheld by My righteous, omnipotent hand."

3. "When through fiery trials thy pathway shall lie,
   My grace, all sufficient, shall be thy supply:
   The flame shall not hurt thee; I only design
   Thy dross to consume and thy gold to refine."

4. "The soul that on Jesus hath leaned for repose
   I will not, I will not desert to its foes;
   That soul, though all hell should endeavor to shake,
   I'll never, no never, no never forsake!"

THE SOLID ROCK

Words: Edward Mote, 1797–1874
Music: William B. Bradbury, 1816–1868

1. My hope is built on nothing less
   Than Jesus' blood and righteousness;
   I dare not trust the sweetest frame,
   But wholly lean on Jesus' name.

   Refrain:
   > On Christ, the solid Rock, I stand—
   > All other ground is sinking sand,
   > All other ground is sinking sand.

2. When darkness veils His lovely face,
   I rest on His unchanging grace;
   In ev'ry high and stormy gale,
   My anchor holds within the veil.

3. His oath, His covenant, His blood
   Support me in the whelming flood;
   When all around my soul gives way,
   He then is all my hope and stay.

4. When He shall come with trumpet sound,
   O may I then in Him be found;
   Dressed in His righteousness alone,
   Faultless to stand before the throne.

APPENDIX FIVE

QUESTIONS TO CONSIDER WHEN EVALUATING
CONTEMPORARY CHRISTIAN MUSIC

This is a summary of a few of the questions that need to be addressed when trying to discern if CCM truly stands up to biblical principles. NOTE: These questions are to be applied as an evaluation of the musical styles and techniques of CCM only; they are not to be used for an evaluation of the lyrics.

1. In what manner do CCM musical techniques demonstrate a set apart lifestyle to the unbeliever? (2 Cor. 6:17)

2. How do the musical styles of CCM model a transformed life of those performing it? How do sensual musical and vocal techniques illustrate a denial of our flesh? (Rom. 12:2; Tit. 2:12)

3. In what way do breathiness and other sultry vocal techniques exhibit godliness? (1 Tim. 6:11; 2 Pet. 3:11)

4. What does the world say about the many styles of CCM? (John 15:19a) What does God say? (Luke 16:15; James 4:4)

5. How do the various musical styles of contemporary Christian music teach such scriptural truths as: 1) "Love not the world," 2) "be not conformed to this world," and 3) "Be holy, for I [God] am holy"? (1 John 2:15; Rom. 12:2; 1 Pet. 1:15–16 NKJV)

6. In what manner is God's glory and righteousness shown forth through musical techniques that cause listeners to sway their hips or perform other sexually suggestive movements? (1 Pet. 1:15–16; 1 Cor. 9:27)

7. Which specific, identifiable, sensual music techniques and/or styles used in CCM encourage listeners to demonstrate the biblical principle (and fruit of the Spirit) of self-control? (Gal. 5:22–24; 2 Pet. 1:5–9)

8. How do the various rhythms used in contemporary Christian music contribute to personal sanctification and Paul's exhortation to "discipline" and bring our bodies "under subjection"? (Tit. 2:12; 1 Pet. 1:15–16; 1 Cor. 9:27)

9. In what way do the musical styles of CCM *fully* comply with Scripture's admonition to sing "spiritual (non-carnal) songs" that don't appeal to the flesh, as revealed through movements the body naturally wants to make? (Eph. 5:19; Col. 3:16)

10. How do sensual music techniques used in CCM demonstrate that our lives are a "living sacrifice, *holy*, acceptable unto God"? (Rom. 12:1, emphasis mine)

ENDNOTES

Chapter One
1. Rom. 7:14, 18, 25; 8:1, 5–8, 13; Gal. 5:16–17, 19–21, 24.
2. "lewdness" NKJV = "lasciviousness" KJV. Mark 7:20–23; 2 Cor. 12:20–21; Gal. 5:19–21.

Chapter Two
1. See Isa. 23:15b and Prov. 5:3; also view the video, "The Sound of Music," from the seminar, *The Language of Music,* by Dr. Frank Garlock. (Majesty Music, PO Box 6524, Greenville, SC 29606. 1-800-334-1071.)
2. David Pogue and Scott Speck, *Classical Music for Dummies* (Foster City, CA: IDG Books Worldwide, Inc., 1997) 274.

Chapter Three
1. Rom. 13:1–7; Tit. 3:1; 1 Pet. 2:13–15.
2. *The American Heritage Dictionary*, p. 107. Copyright © 1983 by Houghton Mifflin Company. Adapted and reproduced by permission from *The American Heritage Dictionary, Second Paperback Edition.*
3. 2 Cor. 6:17.
4. See author's book, *Oh, Be Careful Little Ears* (Enumclaw, WA: WinePress Publishing, 1997) 51–55.

5. Tim Fisher and Dan Sweatt, *Praise Him in Joyful Song:* "Contemporary Christian Music" audio cassette, side five. (Sacred Music Services, Inc., PO Box 17072, Greenville, SC 29606. 1-800-767-4326.)

6. Dan Peters and Steve Peters, *Why Knock Rock?* (Minneapolis: Bethany House, 1984) 13.

7. Richard Aquila, *That Old Time Rock and Roll, A Chronicle of an Era, 1954–1963* (New York: Schirmer Books, 1989) 3.

8. Ibid., p. 5, originally quoted from *The Sound of the City: The Rise of Rock and Roll,* Charlie Gillett (New York: Dutton, 1970) 30–31.

9. Gal. 5:22–23; 2 Pet. 1:5–6.

10. Frank Zappa, "The Oracle Has It All Psyched Out," *LIFE* June 28, 1968: 85.

11. David A. Noebel, *The Legacy of John Lennon: Charming or Harming a Generation?* (Nashville: Thomas Nelson, Inc., 1982) 81.

12. Rom. 12:1–2; Tit. 2:12; 1 Pet. 1:14–16.

Chapter Four

1. Dr. Frank Garlock, *The Language of Music* video series, part three: "The Sound of Music." See also, Tim Fisher and Dan Sweatt, *Praise Him in Joyful Song* audio cassette discussions, side five: "Contemporary Christian Music."

2. Exod. 8:19.

3. Lev. 19:31; 20:6, 27; Deut. 18:9–12; 1 Sam. 15:23.

4. Num. 22:28–30.

5. John 3:16; Rom. 1:16; Eph. 2:8; 2 Tim. 3:15.

6. Rom. 6:1–8:17; Gal. 5:16–17.

7. 2 Chron. 20:19; 30:21; Neh. 12:42; Ps. 98:4; 150:5.

8. 2 Cor. 5:17; Gal. 6:15.

9. 2 Sam. 6:14–16; Ps. 149:3; 150:4.

10. 2 Chron. 5:11–6:3; 7:1–6.

11. Tim Fisher, *Harmony at Home* (Greenville, SC: Sacred Music Services, 1999) 138–148. Also see *Measuring the Music,* by

John Makujina (Salem, OH: Schmul Publishing Co., 2000) 242–252. Refer to Appendix One, "Books/Booklets," for further information.

12. NKJV: Mark 7:20–23; 2 Cor. 12:20–21; Gal. 5:19–21; Eph. 4:17–19.

13. John 4:5–42; Acts 17:16–34.

14. Matt. 16:24; Rom. 6:11–14, 19; 12:1–2; 2 Tim. 1:9; Tit. 1:8; 2:12; 1 Pet. 1:13–16.

15. This list is not exhaustive: Secular authors: *The Closing of the American Mind,* Allan Bloom (New York: Simon and Schuster, 1987); *Amusing Ourselves to Death,* Neil Postman (New York: Penguin Group, 1985); *The Secret Power of Music,* David Tame (New York: Destiny Books, 1984); *That Old Time Rock and Roll, A Chronicle of an Era,* Richard Aquila (New York: Schirmer Books, 1989); *Sound Effects, Youth, Leisure, and the Politics of Rock 'n' Roll,* Simon Frith (New York: Pantheon Books, 1978); *Music and Trance,* Gilbert Rouget (Chicago: University of Chicago Press, 1985); Christian authors: *Music in the Balance,* Frank Garlock and Kurt Woetzel (Greenville, SC: Majesty Music, 1992; 1996); *Harmony at Home,* Tim Fisher (Greenville, SC: Sacred Music Services, Inc., 1999). Also refer to the audio tape series, *Praise Him in Joyful Song,* "Conversations on Church Music" (side five, "Contemporary Christian Music"), Tim Fisher and Dan Sweatt (Sacred Music Services, Inc., 1990).

16. See this entire passage about following Jesus: Luke 14:25–35. Also reread footnote A, under statement number one in the text. Emotionalism plays a huge part in decisions made. Yet, the decisions were not life changing in the final analysis.

17. 1 Cor. 3:8–15.

18. Ps. 14:1–3; Rom. 3:10–12.

19. Matt. 3:2; Mark 1:15; 6:12; Luke 13:3, 5; Acts 3:19; Rom. 3:20; Gal. 3:24.

20. Matt. 5:13.

21. Read *Eternity in Their Hearts*, by Don Richardson (Ventura, CA: Regal Books, a Division of Gospel Light, 1981).
22. Rom. 13:14; 2 Cor. 7:1; Gal. 5:13, 16–24; Tit. 2:12.
23. Garlock, *The Language of Music* video series, part five: "The Effects of Music." Also refer to the audio cassette discussion, "Contemporary Christian Music" from the series, *Praise Him in Joyful Song*, by Tim Fisher and Dan Sweatt.
24. Matt. 16:24–25; Mark 8:34–35; John 3:16; Rom. 10:9–13; 12:1–2; 1 John 2:15–16.
25. Also: Eph. 5:8–11, particularly verse 10; Rom. 12:1–2; Gal. 6:4; 1 Thess. 5:21.
26. There are many books available about the New Age Movement and its philosophy. Here are a couple of suggestions: *A Crash Course on the New Age Movement*, Elliot Miller (Grand Rapids, MI: Baker Book House, 1993); *Dark Secrets of the New Age*, Texe Marrs (Wheaton, IL: Crossway Books, 1987).
27. The books included in the book list of number 15 (above) record these admissions and/or observations.
28. Rom. 6:16; Eph. 1:4; 1 Pet. 1:14–16; 2 Pet. 3:11.
29. Mal. 3:6; Tit. 1:2; Heb. 6:18.
30. Also see Rom. 14:13–21; Eph. 5:1–18; 2 Tim. 2:22.
31. Rom. 6:19.
32. 2 Cor. 11:23–33.
33. Exod. 20:14.
34. Heb. 11:25.
35. Rom. 8:13 NKJV. Also see 1 Pet. 2:11.
36. Also refer to Richard Aquila's book, *That Old Time Rock and Roll*, pp. 3–11.
37. Rom. 6:19; Gal. 5:23; Tit. 1:7–8; 2:2,12; 2 Pet. 1:5–7.
38. Mark Kurlansky, "Voodoo Heart," *Travel Holiday* November 1996: 70–74.
39. Michael Ventura, "Hear That Long Snake Moan," *Whole Earth Review* Spring 1987: 34–35. Reprinted from *Shadow Dancing*, by Michael Ventura (published by Jeremy P. Tarcher, © 1985 by Michael Ventura). NOTE: In no way do I endorse

this magazine; however, this crude article is very enlightening about rock music's very pagan and sinful origins.

40. Tim Fisher's book, *Harmony 'at Home* (Greenville, SC: Sacred Music Services, 1999) has some very revealing quotes from secular artists (see pp. 94–97). Also view the video, *What's Wrong with Christian Rock?* by Jeff Godwin. (The Rock Ministries, PO Box 2181, Bloomington, IN 47402).

41. Jeff Godwin, *Rock and Roll Voodoo* audio cassette.

42. 1 John 4:1–3.

43. 1 Sam. 13:14; 1 Kings 14:8.

44. Suzanne Haïk-Vantoura, *The Music of the Bible Revealed* (Berkeley, CA: BIBAL Press, 1991). Recordings of this music are also available.

45. 1 Cor. 2:16.

46. Prov. 3:5, paraphrased.

47. Rom. 12:1–2; Eph. 5:10; 1 Thess. 5:21.

48. Also see 1 John 2:3–5.

Chapter Five

1. Rom. 7:14–25.

2. Rom. 8:1–13; 13:14; Eph. 4:22.

3. Rom. 12:2; Rom. 13:14; Eph. 4:24; Col. 3:10.

4. Rom. 8:13 NKJV; Rom. 13:14; Col. 3:5.

5. Tit. 2:12; 1 Pet. 1:15–16; 2 Pet. 3:11.

6. 1 Cor. 3:1.

7. Rom. 13:14 NKJV.

8. Gal. 5:22–23.

Chapter Six

1. Exod. 29:1–35; Lev. 8:1–36; Num. 8:21–22.

2. Rom. 13:1–7; 1 Tim. 2:1–3; 1 Pet. 2:13–15.

3. Gen. 41:14.

4. Esther 5:1.

5. John 4:23–24.

6. Acts 10:34; Rom. 2:11; James 2:1.
7. Ps. 139:23; Prov. 21:2; Jer. 17:9; 20:12; Acts 15:8.
8. Prov. 9:10.
9. John 6:60–66.
10. Matt. 7:13–14, 21–23; Luke 13:22–30.
11. John 6:60.

Chapter Seven

1. Tipper Gore, *Raising PG Kids in an X-rated Society* (Nashville: Abingdon Press, 1987; NY: Bantam Books, 1988). While Mrs. Gore is correct about the vileness of some secular rock lyrics, her message does not address rock music's carnal appeal to the flesh; nor does it address the inappropriateness of "Christian" rock music for worship or personal sanctification.
2. Prov. 4; 22:6; Matt. 5:6, 8; 1 Pet. 1:15–16.
3. NOTE: God *is* interested in how we worship and serve Him. Notice the precise details He gave for the Tabernacle in the Old Testament (Exod. 25:1–31:18), as well as principles set forth in the New Testament (Matt. 28:18–20; John 4:24; Rom. 10:17; 12:1; 1 Cor. 11:17–34; 14:26–40; Eph. 5:19; Col. 3:16).
4. John 14:23; Rom. 8:9–10; Gal. 2:20; Col. 1:27.
5. Judg. 17:6 NKJV.
6. Prov. 2:2; 3:13; 4:5; 4:7; 5:1; 10:23; 16:16; 17:24; 23:23.

Chapter Eight

1. Rom. 14:11–12; 2 Cor. 5:10.
2. Matt. 24:12; 2 Thess. 2:3; 2 Tim. 4:3–4.
3. The world "loves its own": John 15:19a; the world "hates" true believers and what they stand for: Mark 13:13; Luke 6:22; John 15:18–19; 1 John 3:13. Even more strongly, James 4:4 states, ". . . know ye not that the friendship of the world

is enmity with God? whosoever therefore will be *a friend of the world is the enemy of God*" (emphasis mine).
4. Matt. 11:6; Rom. 9:33; 1 Pet. 2:7–8. Also see above Scriptures concerning the world's hatred for believers.
5. Rom. 11:25 NKJV.
6. Judg. 17:6; 21:25.
7. Ps. 106:15.
8. Ps. 45:7; 97:10a; Prov. 8:13; Amos 5:14–15a; Rom. 12:9.

Chapter Nine
1. *Oh, Be Careful Little Ears*, p. 96.
2. Ps. 106:15. (This entire Psalm, though referring to Israel, should be a solemn warning to us as Christians.)
3. Rom. 13:14 NKJV.
4. Rom. 12:2.
5. Rom. 7:7–11 NKJV.
6. Recommended by Dr. Jim Logan of the International Center for Biblical Counseling, Sioux City, Iowa.
7. 2 Cor. 6:17; Tit. 2:11–12; James 1:27; 4:4; 1 John 2:15–17.
8. Tit. 2:11–12.
9. Jer. 17:9.
10. Matt. 5:6.
11. Rev. 3:15–16.
12. Matt. 25:21, 23 NKJV.

BIBLIOGRAPHY

Aquila, Richard. *That Old Time Rock and Roll, A Chronicle of an Era, 1954–1963.* New York, NY: Schirmer Books. A Division of Macmillan, Inc., 1989.

Fisher, Tim. *Harmony at Home.* Greenville, SC: Sacred Music Services, Inc., 1999.

Fisher, Tim and Sweatt, Dan. *Praise Him in Joyful Song: Conversations on Church Music.* (Audio tape series.) Greenville, SC: Sacred Music Services, Inc., 1990.

Garlock, Frank and Woetzel, Kurt. *Music in the Balance.* Greenville, SC: Majesty Music, 1992.

Garlock, Frank, Ph.D. *The Language of Music.* (Video series.) Greenville, SC: Majesty Music, 1992.

Godwin, Jeff. *What's Wrong with Christian Rock?* (Video.) Bloomington, IN: The Rock Ministries, 1992.

———. *Rock and Roll Voodoo.* (Audio tape.) Bloomington, IN: The Rock Ministries.

Kavanaugh, Patrick. *A Taste for the Classics.* Nashville, TN: Sparrow Press, 1993.

Kurlansky, Mark. "Voodoo Heart." *Travel Holiday.* November 1996: 70–74.

Makujina, John. *Measuring the Music*. Salem, OH: Schmul Publishing Co., 2000.

Noebel, David A. *The Legacy of John Lennon: Charming or Harming a Generation?* Nashville, TN: Thomas Nelson, Inc. © Summit Ministries, 1982.

Peters, Dan and Peters, Steve. *Why Knock Rock?* Minneapolis: Bethany House, 1984.

Pogue, David and Speck, Scott. *Classical Music for Dummies*. Foster City, CA: IDG Books Worldwide, Inc., 1997.

Strong, James. *The New Strong's Exhaustive Concordance of the Bible*. Nashville: Thomas Nelson, 1984.

The American Heritage Dictionary. Copyright © 1983 by Houghton Mifflin Company. Adapted and reproduced by permission from *The American Heritage Dictionary, Second Paperback Edition*.

Ventura, Michael. "Hear That Long Snake Moan." *Whole Earth Review*. Spring 1987: 28–43.

Zappa, Frank. "The Oracle Has it all Psyched Out." *LIFE*. June 1968: 82–91.

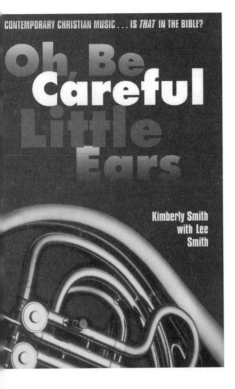

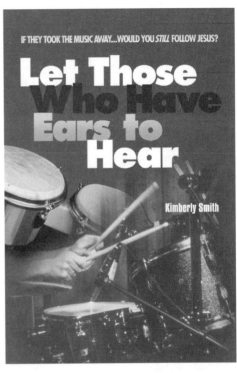

A brief overview of the development of Christian music from both historical and biblical perspectives. Shows why CCM is not biblical. Also includes information about New Age and pop music.

144 pages $9.99

Continues the discussion about CCM—*why* it is a controversial issue and its resulting consequences to the Church. Fifty excuses used to defend CCM are biblically refuted.

216 pages $10.99

To Order

Have your credit card ready and call
(877) 421-READ (7323)

or send $9.99 for *Oh, Be Careful Little Ears*
or $10.99 for *Let Those Who Have Ears to Hear*
plus shipping & handling**
to
WinePress Publishing
PO Box 428
Enumclaw, WA 98022

Online orders: www.winepresspub.com

**S&H: your choice—$4.95–USPS 1st Class
$3.95–USPS Book Rate
Add $1.00 S&H for each additional book ordered